LEARNING TO LIVE WITH THE ONE YOU LOVE

JIM SMITH

TYNDALE HOUSE PUBLISHERS
WHEATON, ILLINOIS

Library of Congress Cataloging-in-Publication Data

Smith, Jim, date
    Learning to live with the one you love / Jim Smith.
        p.   cm.
    ISBN 0-8423-0501-7
    1. Marriage—United States.   2. Marriage—Religious aspects—
Christianity.   I. Title.
HQ734.S7285   1991
646.7'8—dc20   91-23757

To JAN,
my wife of more than thirty years,
who from the beginning
possessed an uncommon sense
about marriage.

CONTENTS

FOREWORD

A sardonic sage once quipped, "Horse sense is what keeps horses from betting on people." I've always winced at the use of the phrase "common sense," since real *sense* seems to be anything but *common*.

Since 1979, I have spent in excess of twelve thousand hours working with couples in and out of marriage. At least two thousand hours were spent preparing couples for marriage in an extensive premarital counseling program. Other hours were spent with couples who were contemplating divorce or with individuals who were trying to survive a divorce.

The rest of the time was spent with many couples who, in the midst of marriage, were struggling valiantly to create or sustain a meaningful life together.

Many of these couples were dealing with serious issues that involved various degrees of pathology in either or both partners. Substance abuse; wife battering; incest; severe codependency; verbal, emotional, and physical abuse; and other such problems were taking their toll in some of these relationships. There were (and are) no easy answers for these deeply wounded couples, and, apart from God's healing grace, some of them would not have made it.

In many cases, the couples I met seemed to lack a commonsense understanding of what marriage is, as well as what it can promise and deliver. In many cases, their expectations and agendas for marriage were sheer nonsense. Some had read a book or an article and suddenly thought they had a revelation about what their marriage ought to be.

I tried to listen carefully. Often, I was able to get the

couples to relax and see things in a new perspective by simply saying, "It sounds to me like you have a severe case of the normals!" The fact that men and women are different in so many ways seemed to have escaped them entirely.

There was a time not so long ago when all the answers seemed clear. Everyone knew which was the weaker sex. Analyzed in political power and bodily brawn, wasn't it obvious? Turn-of-the-century scientists produced learned tracts solemnly warning against an excess of exercise or education for girls. Too much activity or thinking would divert needed blood from their reproductive systems.

Pseudoscientists meticulously measured human brains and found women's wanting. And when the new science of intelligence testing turned up repeated and systematic superiority among girls, researchers kept tinkering with the tests until they produced the *right* results.

Then we had a backlash in the other direction. Feminist scholarship of the 1970s insisted with equal ideological fervor that, apart from the obvious dimorphism of human beings (that is, half being male and half female), there were no real intellectual differences between the sexes.

The liberation movement pronounced loudly that disparities in mental abilities, emotional makeup, attitudes, and even many physical skills were merely the product of centuries of male domination and male-dominated interpretation. More nonsense!

Slowly, in bits and pieces that are still the subject of lively debate, science has been learning more and more about the finer points of how men and women differ;

more about their physiology, psychology, and the inter-
play between them, along with the subtle ways society
influences both. We should be grateful to these researchers, and perhaps as time passes they will shed more and
more light on the *nature versus nurture* issues.

This book is not an attempt to capture the latest in that
research. Though I have quoted some interesting observations and possible conclusions from many of these
sources, this book offers commonsense observations
about men and women today. How they got that way
and whether or not they should be that way will continue to be part of the ongoing debate.

My observations are about women and men in general.
They are not to be taken as universals, for there are obvious exceptions. As a counselor, I have had to work with
men and women where they are, as they are, and who
they are, and not as someone may have declared that
they *ought to be.*

I have also sought to bring the best of biblical and psychological insight to bear on these issues, along with commonsense observations from both of these sources. I have
tried to be sensitive to basic issues of interest to young
couples but also to provide ample thought-provoking
material for older couples stopping in for a ten thousand–
mile checkup.

Marriage is the most basic and vital organization created by God, and the success of our society truly hinges
upon the success of this union. The marriage of a man
and woman is a sacred bond, but it can also be the source
of our greatest happiness and joy. Given such realities,
doesn't it make sense to do whatever it takes to maintain
the health and vitality of this institution?

Whether you have come to this book as a newlywed, as

a young person examining your own expectations for a successful marriage, or as a veteran of married life, it is my sincere hope that you will find a lot of *uncommon sense* within these pages.

Jim Smith
Dallas, Texas

ACKNOWLEDGMENTS

I would like to extend my sincere thanks to all the people who have encouraged me in the writing and preparation of this work.

Thanks to Dr. Jim Nelson Black for his able assistance in the preparation of the manuscript; to my esteemed colleagues, Kristan Kirkpatrick, Russell Jonas, and Dr. Sally St. Clair for their encouragement and creative stimulation; and to Dr. Wendell Hawley, senior vice president at Tyndale House Publishers, who offered me the inspiration and the opportunity to undertake this exceptional challenge.

Special thanks to Craig Millis who, in addition to reading and critiquing the manuscript, has been a longtime and valued friend. And thanks to all those writers and teachers who have helped to develop my own interest in and understanding of these issues.

ONE

CAUTION: THIS MARRIAGE MAY BE HAZARDOUS TO YOUR HEALTH

As a counselor, I hear a lot of stories about unfulfilled expectations in marriage. A fellow came into my office one day and said, "You know, when I got married, marriage was an ideal. Now, it has turned into an ordeal, and I am here looking for a *new* deal."

Another young man came to me and said, "Well, when I first got married, Jim, everything was wonderful; but as my wife and I were leaving the church . . ."

I also remember the middle-aged wife who said, "You know if my husband *really* loved me, he would have married somebody else!"

And there was the man who said, "I think marriage is a three-ring circus. First comes the engagement ring, then comes the wedding ring, and then comes the suffer-ring."

Perhaps the most sardonic of all is the man who said to his clergyman, "Reverend, you have got to do something about our marriage."

"What do you have in mind?" the preacher asked.

"Well, I want it annulled," said the man.

1

"Annulled? You know that's impossible; marriage is permanent. You took her for better or for worse!"

"That's just it," the man replied, "she's so much worse than I took her for."

Beyond the humor and the irony of such stories is an element of truth we all recognize. Human relationships of any kind are often difficult; but marriage, because it represents a promise of lifetime commitment and companionship between man and woman, is apparently the most difficult of all.

That's why Howard Whitman wrote, "It takes guts to stay married. There will be many crises between the wedding day and the golden anniversary. The people who make it are heroes."

War and Peace

Clearly the war is going on, but there seem to be fewer heroes of the kind Whitman describes. Anyone walking past the newsstand during the last decade could not help noticing all the magazine covers declaring the war between the sexes. Both men and women seem confused.

I recently saw a card that expressed both the confusion and anger of many women. On the front of the card, it said: "First, he said he liked independent women, so I played it cool. Then he said he liked romantic women, so I played it hot. And then he said he liked passive women, so I played it weak. Then he said he liked strong women . . ." Then I opened the card, and it said, "So I crushed his head."

The Scripture says, "It is not good that man should be alone" (Genesis 2:18). But we have to wonder how many people still believe that. By their behavior outside of marriage and by their actions within it, millions of men and women are saying they're not so sure. They say, "Maybe so, maybe not, but being alone is better than what I have experienced in marriage."

The newspapers are telling us that one out of every two marriages in this country will end in divorce. We also know that there has been a 500 percent increase in divorce in America since 1960. Adding to the statistics is the high percentage of men and women who go through more than three divorces in a lifetime, as if marriage were simply a means of celebrating a temporary relationship.

Some popular psychologists have proclaimed this the era of "serial marriages," seeing this practice as a healthy new trend in society. And some social scientists see multiple marriages as a normal evolutionary process. Nonsense! I wonder if the sociologists also have a term for the grief and anguish that accompany divorce.

A hundred years ago the divorce rate in the U.S. was only .5 per 1,000 people; at the turn of the century it was up to .7 per 1,000; in 1950 it was 2.6. That represents a total of just 33,000 divorces in the year 1890 compared to 385,114 divorces in 1950. By 1990 the annual total had jumped to just short of 2 million.

Even in 1975 the divorce rate in this country (what statisticians call the "crude" rate) was 4.9 per 1,000 people (twice that of England), and in 1988 it was 4.8. While there were 2,389,000 marriages in 1988, there were 1,183,000 divorces. You don't have to be brilliant to figure out what that means. There was one divorce for every two marriages in the United States.

Unfortunately, we don't need the divorce statistics to know that the institution of marriage is in serious trouble. The evidence is everywhere. Magazines and newspapers are full of the stories. We see the news on television, or we see it happening to the couple down the block, the people next door, maybe even in our own families. In the 1990s, no one is untouched by divorce.

When we see such carnage all around us, we simply have to ask, Is marriage becoming obsolete? Perhaps we should have a little warning label stenciled on our marriage licenses: "Caution: This marriage may be hazardous to your health."

The sad condition of marriage in this decade is obviously the result of the crazy changes we've seen in our world over the past sixty years or so. While some sociologists seem to want us to believe it is a positive change—breaking down ancient stereotypes and bondage to archaic rituals—the fact is that as a society we have lost touch with the deeper values of our faith and our culture.

The Certainty of Change

No matter how we look at the crisis of divorce in America, one thing is certain: things have changed, and not necessarily for the better. Life was a little simpler in the old days.

If we could go back to the time of the Neanderthal man, Ug of Urgh, say about 50,000 B.C., we might hear Ug say, in his guttural voice: "Me man, you woman. Me hunt, fish, fight. You cook, keep kids, make clothes, keep mouth shut."

Or journey forward to Puritan England, when Squire Thickwit is heard to say: "Elizabeth, it hath been said thou hast been seen out upon the streets again today. Thou knowest a woman's place is by the hearth. If thou persisteth in this outrage of decency and order, I must indeed take away thy shoes."

Or leap to the 1970s and hear that ever-popular bigot and male chauvinist, Archie Bunker, proclaim: "The only thing that holds a marriage together is the husband being big enough to step back and see where his wife is wrong."

George Leonard, author of *Education and Ecstasy* and *The Ultimate Athlete,* observed that "we can orbit the earth, touch the moon, yet this society has not devised a way for man and woman to live together, for seven straight days, with any assurance of harmony" (from *The End of Sex,* J. P. Tarcher, 1982). When we hear such things, we really have to ask ourselves, is there any chance of harmony in marriage? Is there any guarantee that a man and woman can live together in peace?

Virginia Satir, a highly recognized counselor, said, "Marriage is the only contract in the Western Christian world that has no time length, no opportunity for review, and no socially acceptable means of termination." She went on to suggest to the American Psychological Association an "apprentice" period for people contemplating marriage. She proposed a five-year terminal point for all marriages with the option for either renewal or termination of the contract.

As a minister, I am frequently called upon to perform marriages in my church. If Ms. Satir's plan were implemented, the couples who stand before me might be reciting vows such as: "I, Mark, take you, Mary, for five years! Then we will take a look at it."

The Three Stages of Marriage

As I have taught and counseled on the subject of marriage, I have come to the conclusion that most marriages go through three predictable stages. The first is the stage of *enchantment.* Hopefully it starts well before the honeymoon and lasts for a period of time after it. The enchantment may last a couple of weeks or a couple of months. It may even last a couple of years; but one day you wake up and discover you're married to a human being!

Suddenly the courtship is over and the relationship begins. Someone has said that courtship is the maximum time of human deception. Maybe, but at some point the courtship and the enchantment come to a screeching halt—at least temporarily.

It would be comic if it weren't so serious. As you look at this person you thought was such a beautiful, fantastic creature, for the first time you see that this human being actually has faults! But worst of all, those faults irritate you—they make you mad. "How in the world did this happen?" you wonder. Little by little, reality starts to sink in.

After the initial enchantment, all marriages go through a second stage, which is a period of *disenchantment.* This can either be a period of discomfort and growth, or it can be a very dangerous time, depending on how you understand your role as husband or wife and how you feel about marriage. If the disenchantment continues for a long period without being resolved or interrupted, you begin to believe that you have made a huge mistake.

Some people react in horror. They scream, "I married the wrong one!" Or, "I didn't get the right model!" All the war stories you have heard about broken marriages come rushing in on you. You start to think of yourself as a victim, and in some cases you immediately start looking for the exit. "I've got to get out of here. I've got to try again. Somewhere out there is the mate I was really supposed to have. If I don't hurry, it will be too late!"

Some couples grow through this period; others are destroyed by it. Those who endure their stage of disenchantment and learn from it actually move on to greater maturity and happiness. Those who get stuck at this point generally end up on the casualty list. They become the statistics we talked about at the beginning of the chapter.

Every married couple goes through a period of disenchantment, and each deals with it differently. Many factors, including our own parenting and our attitudes about how marriage and family are supposed to work, influence the way we react, but the disenchantment is inevitable. In fact, you can add it to the list of things that are certain in life: *death, taxes,* and *disenchantment in marriage.*

However, we don't want to get stuck at that point. While it is important to be forewarned and to recognize that many of the problems we experience in marriage today are predictable to some degree, we really want to move beyond that stage. What comes later, the third stage, the maturing of the husband-wife relationship into a *healthy marriage* is so much richer and so much better.

Why do I say "healthy" marriage? I think it is universally accepted by most people in the helping professions today—psychologists, psychiatrists, and the like—that most emotionally unhealthy individuals come from unhealthy family backgrounds. That's easy to understand, especially if you believe the Old Testament teaching that the sins of the fathers (and mothers) are visited upon the children (see Exodus 34:7).

Obviously, unhealthy parents will tend to raise unhealthy kids, who will grow up to be unhealthy parents and will keep the cycle going until either God in his infinite mercy interrupts it or until people caught in the cycle get help and break the pattern.

I am not especially interested in tracking the pathology of friction in marriage or even in discovering some formula for perfect harmony. It seems much wiser to recognize that strife is inevitable and that if we plan to be happy, we will have to learn to deal with it. To grow into the third stage of marriage, to a place of balance and security, we must acquire the skills necessary to maintain love and security in the home. Isn't that what we all want?

The world throws enough pain and hurt at us; we don't want our homes to become battlefields. Instead, home should be a place of shelter. We should be able to come home from our responsibilities and activities to find peace and contentment at home.

Ideals, Expectations, and Reality

While conducting a marriage enrichment seminar in a cold northern state a few years ago, I noticed that one particular woman was taking copious notes throughout my entire presentation. Of course, I was flattered. A speaker always feels complimented when he sees that somebody feels that what he is saying is worth writing down. This lady just kept writing and writing.

When I spoke to her at the end of the seminar, however, I discovered that she had been doing some creative writing. In her notes, she had given a curious slant to what I had been saying that weekend. Here's what she wrote.

She had made two columns on her paper. At the top of the first column was written, "What Every Man Expects When He Gets Married." Across from that she had written, "What He Gets." On the second page she had done the same thing from the woman's perspective.

Under "What Every Man Expects," she had written, "The ideal wife." In my seminar, I had said that a lot of men today seem to want a combination of Linda Evans, Bo Derek, Mother Teresa, and Margaret Thatcher. Unfortunately, women like that don't exist. Every woman wants a man with the qualities of Robert Redford, Billy Graham,

Superman, and George Bush all rolled into one. Obviously, we all have to make some trade-offs!

So my listener wrote that a man expects a wife who:

> Is always beautiful and cheerful.
> Could have married a movie star, but wants only you.
> Has hair that never needs curlers or a beauty shop.
> Has beauty that won't run in a rainstorm.
> Is never sick; she's just allergic to jewelry and fur coats.
> Insists that moving the furniture by herself is good for her figure.
> Is an expert in cooking and cleaning house and fixing the car or television set.
> She's an expert in painting the house and keeping quiet.
> Her favorite hobbies are mowing the lawn and shoveling snow.
> She hates charge accounts, and her favorite expression is, "What can I do for you, Dear?"
> She thinks you have Einstein's brain and look like Mr. America, and she says she loves you because you're so sexy.

Then across from that, under the column "What He Gets," she had written:

> She speaks 140 words a minute with gusts up to 180.
> She was once a model . . . for a totem pole.
> She is known as a light eater: as soon as it gets light, she starts eating.
> Where there is smoke, there she is, cooking.
> No matter what she does, her hair looks like an explosion in a steel wool factory.

The last time she used a broom was to fly somewhere.
If you get lost, open your wallet. She'll find you.
She fights with the neighbors just to keep in practice
  until you get home.
She lets you know you only have two faults: everything you say, and everything you do.

In my comments during the seminar, I had said something about the irony between the first days and the last
days of a troubled marriage. I had said, "It's fun to go to
weddings, isn't it? I go to quite a few; I perform quite a
few, in fact. Sometimes I think of those starry-eyed
couples, so in love, so infatuated with each other. Sometimes you just have to wonder, how can anything that
starts out so wonderful end so tragically?

On page two of her notes, my listener was a little more
poetic. Under "What Every Woman Expects," she had
written:

The Ideal Husband

One well groomed and charming.
  A dashing one, too.
Could have married great women,
  but desires only you.

No five o'clock shadow
  ever crosses his face.
He's always dressed in the latest,
  each hair in its place.

He's never sick; he's a tower of
  strength all for you.

He's just allergic to golf clubs
. . . and snowmobiles, too.

He insists his love not strain herself
in any way.
He hangs up his clothes,
and does the dishes each day.

He's an expert in making
and managing money,
And he's generous when giving
such gifts to his honey.

He rules his well-behaved children
with hand firm and fair.
He's a painter, a plumber,
an expert at lawn care.

He's a great conversationalist,
well-versed in all things.
He's a right cheerful fellow;
he whistles and sings.

He's always asking,
"Is there something you'd like to do?"
He loves you so much,
just because you're you!

So across from that, under "What She Gets," my listener
had written, still in verse:

He grunts: once if by land,
two if by sea,
while glued to his chair
by the color TV.

His hair, what's left,
  needs a brush and shampoo;
and his chest? Well, it sunk,
  irretrievably, too.

He snaps at the children
  and kicks the poor dog.
After wolfing his supper,
  he sleeps like a log.

He expects T-bone steak
  as his bill of fare,
but the budget allows
  only filet of mare.

The paint is all chipped
  and the porch is sagging.
You mention it once
  and get walloped for nagging.

He needs one night each week
  to go out with the boys.
He thinks speedboats and cycles
  are his well-deserved toys.

When you'd like to find out
  if he loves you or no,
He just shrugs and says,
  "I'm still here aren't I? So?"

At the bottom of the page she had written:

How amazing to me is God's wonderful plan.
He takes imperfect woman and imperfect man,
two quite different persons, and when he's done,
they're molded and formed by his hands into one.

A wedding is but a first foundation block,
but marriage goes on building rock upon rock
until you're melded together through trial and test,
while he makes good things better, and better things best.

That's what Mary Pelto was writing while I was speaking. She's a very creative woman. Thanks, Mary, for letting me share your creativity with others.

The Master Plan

When we begin to look at issues concerning the family, it is always good to start by examining what the Bible has to say. What did God have in mind when he designed marriage? Did you ever wonder about the "divine design"?

I think it's interesting that you don't have to turn very far in the Bible to find the answer. It's in the first chapter of the first book.

The family is the first institution that God ever put together. He put it together before government. He put it together before the church. God obviously intended for marriage to be the foundation of all society and culture. Genesis 1:26-28 reads:

> Then God said, "Let us make a man—someone like ourselves, to be the master of all life upon the earth and in the skies and in the seas."
> So God made man like his Maker.
> Like God did God make man;
> Man and maid did he make them.
> And God blessed them and told them, "Multiply and fill the earth and subdue it; you are masters of the fish and birds and all the animals." (TLB)

In the second chapter of Genesis, God saw that man was lonely. Beginning with verse 18, it says, "And the Lord God said, 'It isn't good for man to be alone; I will make a companion for him, a helper suited to his needs'" (TLB). Then in verses 20-23 we read:

> But still there was no proper helper for the man. Then the Lord God caused the man to fall into a deep sleep, and took one of his ribs and closed up the place from which he had removed it, and made the rib into a woman, and brought her to the man. "This is it!" Adam exclaimed. "She is part of my own bone and flesh! Her name is 'woman' because she was taken out of a man." (TLB)

The Scripture continues:

> This explains why a man leaves his father and mother and is joined to his wife in such a way that the two become one person. Now although the man and his wife were both naked, neither of them was embarrassed or ashamed. (Genesis 2:24-25, TLB)

God showed Adam and Eve the world he had created for them and explained that he had given them the seed-bearing plants and the fruit trees for food, plus all the other plants and animals in the garden. Then God looked at his creation and saw that it was good, and so ended the sixth day of Creation. I think it is interesting to observe that God rested after he created the institution of marriage. Man and woman were united as one flesh; then God said it was good, and he rested.

Later, in the Gospel of Matthew, Jesus reminded the Pharisees that God "made them male and female," adding, "For this cause shall a man leave father and mother, and shall cleave to his wife: and they twain shall be one flesh" (Matthew 19:4-5, KJV). So there is in Scripture a sense of union in marriage called "oneness." Healthy marriages must center around what God had in mind when he created that "oneness" between a man and a woman.

The Call to Oneness

Every marriage needs a period of adjustment. During this time you begin to look at the situation, your ego, and all the baggage you brought with you to the relationship, and try to determine how you're going to get along on a day-to-day basis.

At this point, many settle into becoming what I call a *functional marriage* (see the following diagram). That is, the husband and wife make contact each day, they live under the same roof, and their lives touch, but there is not much going on between them emotionally.

A diagram of this kind of marriage relationship would have two separate circles, near each other but not really touching. In a functional marriage, each partner performs his or her function. Both people are doing their jobs. They go to work; they take care of the house; they have 2.1 kids; and they pay their taxes.

They may go to church on Sunday and may belong to a number of clubs or do other things together. But, for all practical purposes, they are just two adults under the same roof. They are just doing business.

I suspect that many (perhaps even most) marriages over the past five or six thousand years have been functional marriages. Many marriages throughout history were "arranged." Their roles in society gave certain families special privileges and responsibilities; consequently, the families chose whom their children would marry.

Often the arranged marriages involved important matters of land or position or power. Other times they were merely matters of convenience. But think about it. How would you like to marry somebody your parents chose for you? That's a frightening thought, isn't it?

That is not what the Scripture means when it describes God's divine design for "oneness" between man and woman. Such a marriage is functional and it works, and a lot of people settle for that. But does it make sense to you?

The second two circles are what I suspect some people think God meant when he called for oneness in marriage. These two circles are deeply overlapped, almost.obliterating each other. In psychological terms, this is called an *enmeshed marriage.*

Have you ever known a couple like that? They're never very far apart. It is like "me and my shadow." They are thicker than molasses. They are so knotted together that he can't comb his hair without her permission, and she wouldn't think of going to the store without him. It's kind of sickening, isn't it? At some point, the cute and cuddly wears thin, and what is left is two helpless Siamese twins.

In an enmeshed marriage, you can't tell where one person ends and the other begins. There are no defined boundaries. They have absorbed each other and "become one." I don't think that's at all what God had in mind when he states, "Therefore shall a man leave his father and mother, and shall cleave unto his wife: and they shall be one flesh" (Genesis 2:24, KJV).

Besides the pathological implications of an "enmeshed" marriage, this type of bonding can create enormous problems. This can also happen in the parent-

THREE KINDS OF MARRIAGE

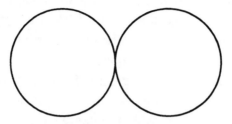

Functional Marriage

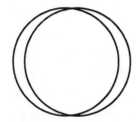

Enmeshed Marriage

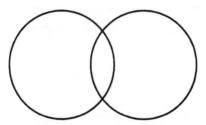

Relational Marriage

ing process. A parent can become enmeshed with the child, or the child can become enmeshed with the parent. This can lead to all kinds of emotional difficulties and codependency problems. We'll touch more on that as we go along. But surely this is not what the Scripture is calling for, either.

A third type of relationship provides a much better balance. As shown in the diagram, the circles for the *relational marriage* overlap, but there is still a large area that is independent. This kind is what I think the Scripture means when it talks about a healthy marriage. This is the model of "oneness" in marriage.

In the relational marriage, a part of the husband remains autonomous, with a distinct place for independence and self-reliance. At the same time, the wife maintains her own distinct boundaries; she knows who she is as a woman. But the husband and wife also have a large area in common where their lives overlap and interact.

In the relational model, each partner has a healthy sense of self-esteem matched by an equal area of healthy cooperation and sharing. And, of course, there is love. Each partner knows what he or she wants from the other. There is a need for growth and commitment on the part of each partner.

Diagrams are never perfect, so I hope you get the idea. The difference between the three diagrams is not in substance, but in degree. They all represent marriages in which a man and woman have made a life commitment to each other; however, the tone of each marriage is remarkably different.

In the functional marriage there is formal sharing but no emotional relationship. In the enmeshed marriage there is profound emotional sharing but no sense of identity, no logical boundaries. But in the relational marriage there is both a healthy sense of each partner's personhood as well as a healthy area of sharing and togetherness. That's what makes a healthy marriage. And modern research confirms it!

Another type of marriage is one that we don't see a lot

of today (but we see enough of it to be concerned). I call it the *hierarchical marriage*. This is the relationship where one partner becomes the supreme ruler of the household and the other partner is merely a satellite.

In some homes it is the father who dominates everyone with an iron hand. The wife merely circulates around the edges, with the children, doing what she is told. That used to be a fairly common pattern in this country some years ago. Many of our grandparents grew up in "patriarchal families" of this type.

More and more today, we are seeing families where the wife and mother is the real power player in the home. This is the "matriarchal family." Mom rules, and you've got this wimp out on the fringes sort of circulating around in orbit with the children. Everything revolves around mother. Dad is not even a factor.

Developing a Healthy Marriage

Somebody once said, somewhat cynically, that home is where, when you go there, they have to let you in. Well, it really should be much more than that, but the saying is true in a sense. Home should be a place of security, love, acceptance, and togetherness.

Our homes should be that kind of environment: shelters of love and companionship, places of hope, healing, and happiness.

Understanding the patterns of healthy marriage and, beyond that, understanding how unhealthy patterns can be broken are really what this book is all about. So much has been written about unhealthiness, it is only fair to focus on the attributes of *healthy* marriages. But since so much of what has been said about marriage is *common nonsense,* we may have to do a little repair work here and there in order to discuss the *uncommon sense* of a healthy marriage.

One of the most memorable statements about love that I have ever read was written by the French author Teihard de Chardin. He writes that when you love people,

> you love them as they are, not as you wish them to be, not as you hope to help them become, but as they are. When you love people, you love them because they are who they are; not loving in order to change them, not loving as a way of remaking them. But loving because you love. When you love people, you love them, warts and all. Not blinding yourself to their faults, not denying their imperfections, but loving in spite of.
>
> Loving another person is to commit oneself, with no guarantee of return. To love another person is to give oneself, with the risk of rejection. To love another person is to reach out in hope of love to awaken love in the heart of the other. Love is not dependent on the nature of the one loved but on the nature of the one who loves. Love is not contingent on the beauty of the loved but on the appreciation of the lover. Love is not conditional on the constancy of the beloved but on the fidelity of the one who loves.
>
> When you love someone, nothing matters half so much as to accept the other person, to reassure one another, to hear and answer each other, to look deeply into the other's soul, and to show your own. To love someone is to affirm that she is worthy, to bid him to live life freely, to leave her with all her freedom intact, to recognize his dignity as a person,

to invite her to grow, to oblige him to be fully what he is, to inspire her to be all that she can be.

I suggest that if somehow, with God's help, we can begin to deal with our basic differences as men and women and not simply deny them; and if we can again begin to recapture and practice the biblical mandate of loving and forgiving; then for the second time in history, we will have discovered fire!

This book is designed to help us do just that.

TWO

SURPRISE! MEN AND WOMEN *ARE* DIFFERENT!

I firmly believe that God said what he meant and meant what he said in the first book of the Bible: it is not good for man or woman to be alone. Something about human nature makes us long for each other; and unless God has specifically called us to celibacy, I believe we are bound to feel incomplete until completed in a harmonious marriage relationship.

But if the evidence says marriage does not work, that half of all marriages end in divorce and heartbreak, what can we do? Is it really worth it? Do we really care? And if so, what can we do to rescue the institution of marriage?

Before going into a broader treatment of these issues and talking about how we can cope with the various problems, I have three suggestions that deserve consideration.

First of all, I suggest that we are going to have to deal with our differences instead of denying them. Despite everything you've heard and read in the last twenty years, men and women are really different. The androgyny movement (that is, the unisex culture) would like us to believe that men and women are essentially the same. In fact, that movement has done us all a great disservice by causing us to believe what is obviously not true: that men and women *are not* different. Talk about nonsense!

Thank God, men and women are distinctly and wonderfully different. Instead of denying that fact, we should be celebrating it! In an article entitled "Marriage Without Regrets: The Differences between Men and Women," a woman writer lists at least ten differences that she has observed. Some of her choices may be debatable, but let me list them. She says:

1. Men tend to see the "whole"; women tend to see the detail.
2. Men tend to be logical. They say, "I think; I know." Women tend to be intuitive. They say, "I feel."
3. Men tend to make decisions; women tend to lack self-assurance.
4. Men tend to be more emotionally calm; women tend to be more emotionally volatile.
5. Men tend to be more goal-oriented; women tend to be more relationship-oriented.
6. Men tend to be objective; that is, direct. Women tend to be subjective; that is, indirect, relating things to themselves.
7. Men tend to be realistic; women tend to be idealistic. Women often verbalize their dreams; men tend to take women too literally at this point.
8. Men tend to be nomadic. This is heightened because they are goal-oriented. Women tend to have roots. This is related to the fact that they are relationship-oriented.
9. Men need respect more than they need love. In

this book I refer to Paul's instructions to women in Ephesians 5 to *respect* their husbands. Women, on the other hand, need love more than respect. Perhaps that is why Paul told husbands to *love* their wives.

10. Men have two basic fears: the fear of being subjugated by a woman and the fear of being found inadequate. Women, the author suggests, have one basic fear: fear of being treated like objects.

As we look at this list, I believe we have to recognize the validity of the author's perspective. However hard we may try to deny it, there are intrinsic and categorical differences between the way men and women think and behave. I have no doubt that socialization and traditional roles have an impact on behavior; but I believe just as strongly that natural behavior and emotional predisposition have helped to shape socialization and tradition.

Feminists like to say that women have only been traditional guardians of the home because men have always made them do it. Again, I say nonsense! I would argue that the emotions, attitudes, genetic makeup, and even the unique shape and appearance of women is evidence that they are uniquely designed as bearers of children, keepers of the home fires, and the gentle half of the human equation.

Of course, they can do other things. Women can head nations and corporations; they can travel in space and climb mountains. But that should never disguise the fact that they are perfectly suited by their unique design to nurture children and to care for the welfare of their families.

Men are not soft and gentle and caring by nature. They

have to learn that after they are tamed. In the wild, men grow tough and insensitive. They like to fight; they hate to shop. They like sports because it's rough and competitive; they hate tea parties because they're soft and emotional.

Women supply the tender side of human nature that is generally missing in men; and men supply the physical strength, the capacity for aggression, and the hard-headed endurance generally missing in women.

The hardness of the male is not a negative quality: it is an absolute necessity. (And that is as true in the 1990s as it was in prehistoric times!) The defender of the home must be able to fight off predators and defeat marauders. So, by nature, men supply physical toughness to complement the women's gentleness. They are two halves of the same equation; when added together, they are $E=mc^2$—powerful!

Beyond these basic points, I also want to highlight two differences between men and women that I have observed, and make some comments about how they work themselves out in human relationships—especially in marriage. The first is the way we talk—communication. The second is the way we feel about closeness—intimacy.

The Way We Talk

First, males and females have distinctly different conversational styles, based both upon gender and cultural conditioning.

Debra Tannen, in her book *You Just Don't Understand*, subtitled *Women and Men in Conversation*, says she believes that women use what she calls "rapport-talk," which is talk intended to signal support, to confirm solidarity, or to indicate that they are simply following the conversation.

Men, on the other hand, tend to use what she calls "report-talk." For most men, talk is primarily a means to preserve independence, to negotiate, and to maintain status in a hierarchical social order.

To illustrate her point, Ms. Tannen tells a story about a misunderstanding between a husband and wife following a car accident, in which the wife had been seriously injured. It seems the wife hated being cooped up in the hospital, so she asked to come home early. Once home, she suffered pain from having to move around a lot. When she complained to her husband, he said, "Well, why didn't you stay in the hospital where you would have been more comfortable?" His remark cut her deeply because it seemed to imply that he did not want her at home.

She did not understand that his question was simply a practical statement that, if she had stayed in the hospital as the doctors had advised, she could have avoided further pain and suffering. He believed his statement was purely practical, nuts and bolts. She believed it was an expression of his feeling that he would have preferred not to have her around. And on and on it goes.

Marriage is the union of one male and one female: at least that's the way it is supposed to be. When they are young, the differences can be alluring; they draw couples together and lead to romance. But once a man and woman get married and set up housekeeping, those same God-given differences can come between them, sometimes seeming more like wedges driving them apart.

We all know about these differences; we even recognize the dangers. Yet in all the lectures and seminars I've attended on marriage and the family, nobody seems to want to deal with this most basic area of conflict in marriage. It is evident that the emotional and psychological differences between men and women are a major source of conflict. So, it makes sense that we should get the differences out in the open and learn how to live with them.

In premarital counseling, I will frequently say to a young couple, "If you have heard nothing else during the five weeks we've been together, I want you to hear this. You are about to marry a member of the opposite sex."

Invariably, they look at me as if I were crazy. They do know they're marrying someone of the opposite sex, of course; but later when they come back for counseling, I get the feeling that they weren't listening. They keep battling over issues that would disappear completely if they would simply recognize that they are two different people—opposite genders.

Before the wedding, they can talk for hours on end, sharing their heart's desires and exploring each other's hopes and dreams in intimate detail. After the wedding, they don't even speak the same language. They used to breathe the same air; now they seem to be on separate planets. Once the courtship is over and the realities of making a living start to intrude, they have to find new ways of communicating with each other. Some make it; but many don't.

The Communication Barrier
Little by little, brick by brick, many young couples start building barriers to intimacy from their wedding day on. Casual words, innocent acts, simple things that they never discuss grow up between them. So month after month, the barriers become fortresses of emotional resistance.

Conversation is a key example. Men, by and large, tend

to talk in generalities. Women, on the other hand, tend to talk in specifics. Next time you go to a party, try listening to the various groups talking. Listen briefly to a group of men, then to a group of women.

Invariably, the men will be talking about vague, general subjects, often avoiding anything that might expose them emotionally, while the women will be going into elaborate detail and sharing feelings and attitudes quite freely.

The men are talking about the savings and loan bailout, the NFL draft, or the problems at city hall. If they start to talk about their golf game or their last business trip, that's about as personal as it gets.

So it goes. Then listen to the women.

Chances are they will be talking about specific individuals and naming names. One woman's daughter just left for college, and she is afraid the child doesn't have a chance of surviving. The daughter doesn't have a declared major yet, and she never even learned how to clean her room!

Another woman is upset because her son has started dating a girl who's not nearly good enough for him; and still another lady wants to share every detail of her last shopping expedition and the wonderful bargains she discovered.

On a practical level, what does this mean? First of all, women want to talk things out in detail. Men absolutely *do not.* Women, you can easily check me out on this. The next time hubby comes home from a business trip, ask him to tell you all about it.

Say, "Honey, tell me all about your trip."

He'll say, "Got a plane, flew to Chicago, stayed at the Hilton, went to meetings, came home." That's it. Sound familiar?

So you say, "I know all that! I want you to tell me all about the trip."

He'll say, "I just did. You weren't listening."

What does the woman want? She wants detail. She wants to know what the flight attendant had on, what her husband ate on the plane, what the taxicab driver said between the airport and the hotel. She wants to know what he had for breakfast, what the waitress was wearing, whether he had a room with a view, the color of the drapes in the hotel room, and anything else he can think of.

Do you think that will satisfy her? Probably not! Then she will expect her husband to tell her what the guest speaker talked about at the banquet, and what his wife looked like. "What were they wearing?" she will ask. "What did you have for dinner? Was there music? How many people showed up?"

The very idea that anybody would even care about such things absolutely blows a man's mind. In marriage and other male-female relationships, women are verbal; men, as a rule, are not. Women like specifics. Men prefer generalities; generalities are safer.

The Way We Disagree

Consider when couples get into a disagreement. What usually happens? For example, a discussion turns into an argument as they're leaving for work. They haggle back and forth for about forty-five seconds as they're going out the door, and then they go their separate ways.

So what does the man do? He immediately blows it off. He thinks, "Well, we've talked about it." But what does the woman do? She spends the whole day chewing on it, reworking it, hashing it over, and thinking about what he said and contemplating what she said. So when hubby comes home, she meets him at the door and says, "Can we talk?"

He senses she's got something on her mind, but he can't imagine what in the world she wants to talk about.

"Talk?" he says. "About what?"

She squints her eyes real small and says, "You know what I'm talking about! I want to talk about what you said this morning."

Now the old boy scratches his head and says, "Oh, that?" He has already forgotten about the whole thing. So he says, "We already talked about that. We spent at least thirty seconds on it this morning as we were going out the door, don't you remember?"

See the difference? She wants to talk it out in detail. He wants to forget it.

Clearing the Air

When women talk something out in detail, somewhere along the line they let go of it. But unless they do this, they keep holding on. Any man who doesn't grasp that is doomed to keep on hitting the same communication wall over and over again. I can tell you that it took me only twenty years to learn this about my wife. Since then I've observed it in most women. There's something that happens in women that doesn't go on in men.

The husband says, "Let's drop it. Let it alone. We've already hacked that thing to pieces." But the wife doesn't see it that way. And if hubby doesn't let her discuss it and clear the air, it will come up again!

That reminds me of the man who said, "When my wife and I get into an argument, she gets historical!"

Is the masculine way of dealing with problems better than the feminine way? No. Each is simply an aspect of their unique personalities and a sign of the distinctive differences between them. But we have to understand those differences if we want to have harmony in marriage. If we do not learn these things about our mates and learn to live with them, we are bound to suffer a lot of unhappi-ness in marriage.

If men and women ever expect to live together in love and understanding, we will have to learn to deal with the differences in our natures and with the different needs and emotions that will otherwise keep us apart.

The Way We Feel about Closeness

The second major difference between men and women is our distinct feelings and thoughts about intimacy. I saw a fascinating report of a research project at Harvard University. Observing the differences between little boys' and little girls' games, researchers were surprised to discover some fundamental differences. For one thing, the girls' games were always shorter than the boys' games. They also noticed that the little boys preferred games with lots of rules. The observer discovered, to her great interest, that the boys appeared to have about as much fun dis-cussing infractions of the rules as they did actually play-ing the game. In the little girls' games, if there was a quarrel, the girls were more likely to end the game rather than risk a fracture in the relationship. The girls appar-ently felt that relationships were more important than rules.

Some other interesting studies reflect on these essential differences. In one set of studies, researchers observed the different reactions of men and women to various pic-tures. In one picture, a man is shown sitting alone. Another picture is of a trapeze artist, a man hanging by his legs on the trapeze bars and touching a woman's hands. In another group of pictures, the people are getting closer and closer together. After examining all the pictures, the men and women were asked to tell stories about the pictures; that is, they were to explain what led up to the incident pictured.

The men and women in these studies seldom told the same kinds of stories. In fact, the reactions were remarkably different. In their stories about the scenes where the people are getting closer and closer, such as the trapeze photo where there is touching, one out of every five men included the possibility of violence in their stories. The women, on the other hand, tended to tell stories involving violence only when the people were alone. The researchers concluded from this that men tend to see danger in closeness while women tend to see danger in separateness and distance.

Obviously, the fact that men fear closeness and women fear distance can create havoc when we try to relate to each other.

It is astonishing how often I have had single women come into therapy saying that they just don't understand men. One young woman came to see me because she was feeling unloved and abandoned by a male friend she thought she knew very well. "We had this wonderful, close, intimate evening," she told me, "but now he hasn't even called me for three weeks. What's going on?"

She was a very attractive young woman. She was afraid something might be wrong with her, but that wasn't the case. The real problem was that her friend thought they had gotten too close too soon, and he panicked. So his disappearing act was just evidence that he was trying to put some distance back in the relationship. A man feels safer with distance. But when the young man put distance back, the woman felt danger. She longed for closeness.

Spending Time Together

One of the ways this difference between the sexes shows up in marriage is in the very different ideas about how evenings should be spent.

The average man comes home believing that, having put in a hard day at work, it is now his God-given right to retire to his castle. He now wishes to enter his castle, pull up the drawbridge, and let the alligators swim in the moat. He is not particularly thrilled when he learns that there are some alligators loose in the castle.

Now a woman's idea of an evening well spent is called "sharing"—in detail. The career woman wants to share her day with her husband—in detail—and the home-maker wants to share war stories from the home front. And what about the woman who has little children at home and has not been out of the house? She has been locked up with the "Viet Cong" all day and can't wait to turn them over to him the minute he walks in the door. She would like to have an adult conversation—in detail—with her husband.

Have you ever noticed that most men think they have spent a meaningful evening at home with their wives if they have simply been under the same roof? No conversation, no dialogue, no give and take, but they're there, in the same place at the same time—he thinks that means "closeness."

I have heard the charge that a man wants his wife to behave more or less like a good golden retriever: that is, she should come around occasionally and pass through the room, letting him acknowledge and pat her. Then she should go on doing whatever she was doing, coming back in about an hour to let him pat and acknowledge her again. If she does that, he feels that he has spent a wonderful, warm evening with her. When she complains, "You never spend any time with me," he's shocked.

"What?" he yells. "I've been home all week." What he needs to understand is that, at least metaphorically, a woman is not a golden retriever, but more like a lap dog. She would like to have more closeness and intimacy.

Another clear difference in the nature of men and women is seen in their friendships. Men tend to build friendships around activities. We have hunting buddies, fishing buddies, bowling buddies, golfing buddies, poker-playing buddies, and the like. Women, on the other hand, tend to build friendships around sharing. They relate to other women who like to talk about all of the emotions and issues they are dealing with in life.

This may explain why some couples have trouble connecting with other couples their age. In some cases the two women can share quite easily, but the men do not have an activity or interest in common. That makes it difficult. In other cases, it may be the other way around; the men have an activity in common, but the women find that they do not feel comfortable sharing with each other. I do not believe either approach is good or bad. But they are different, and I think this sheds new light on how we develop relationships and friendships.

If we attempt to deny these differences instead of dealing with them, we greatly reduce the chance of making marriage meaningful or of keeping the battle of the sexes relatively harmless.

Man's Secret Fear
Most women do not realize how it threatens a man to share his feelings. Women, inherently, want to talk about feelings and emotions. They want to fix things. They want detail. But the result is often surprising. Digging

into a man's feelings to sort things out is threatening to him. He starts to feel he's being treated like a little boy.

Men inherently try to cover up their feelings with cold, rational logic, which tends to make the woman feel as though she has not been heard. But in a happy marriage, couples eventually have to learn how to handle self-disclosure and how to create an environment where both parties can feel comfortable in sharing their deepest feelings and emotions.

With that in mind, let me mention a couple of incentives for open communication in marriage, along with some of the obstacles to it.

First, *learn to get your feelings out in the open.* It would be interesting to know how many men grew up in homes where they were allowed to express their feelings. For most of history, men have had to repress their feelings. They were not allowed to show emotion.

If they expressed feelings of hurt or tenderness, chances are they heard things like: "Real men don't cry. Quit being a sissy. Grow up. Keep your nose to the grindstone, shoulder to the wheel. Keep a stiff upper lip."

What we call the "I" messages were definitely out. So today, men who need to get their feelings out in the open—to express those "I" messages—have a sizable emotional barrier to overcome. Obviously, learning to do that takes time.

Second, *learn to talk even when there is no crisis.* In a lot of marriages, it seems that the only time the husband and wife actually talk to each other is when there is trouble—with the kids, with the dog, with the car, or at the office.

Frankly, just talking about trouble all the time can be a drag. Get to be friends with each other. And find a time to talk that is mutually agreeable. It may be that you will have to *make* time to talk, just like making a business appointment, because if you wait until a good time just comes along, you may wait forever. If you wait to see what kind of time you have left at the end of the day, guess what? There isn't any!

My wife, Jan, and I got into some good habits by sheer accident. I'd like to say we were thoughtful and sensitive and well-organized, but the truth is that we stumbled into them. One of these is that we always go to bed at the same time. She doesn't stay up and watch Johnny Carson while I'm sawing logs. I don't stay up and watch *The Monster that Ate Philadelphia*, or whatever, after she has gone to bed.

Fortunately for our marriage and our friendship, we made a commitment to go to bed very close to the same time. We try to go to bed early enough that we have some time to talk. That has been important for both of us, especially when the kids were young.

Coordinating bedtimes that way isn't easy to do. But at least it gives us some time together when we don't have the general chaos of phones ringing off the wall or kids running through the house. That one habit has given us some wonderful private time together, and I know our marriage has profited from it.

Another good habit we got into was taking walks together. I find that I'm more comfortable talking about important things with my wife when I'm doing something. As a therapist, I can sit right across from somebody and talk openly, eyeball-to-eyeball. But when I'm with my wife, I find it more relaxing to be busy at some activity. Walking is that kind of activity for us. We can talk a little easier about certain sensitive issues. If there is no particular crisis, we just talk about whatever is going on in our lives at that time.

I found that to be true with our kids as well. When our

daughters, Melody and Cindy, were growing up, every Thursday night was family night. Jan and I spent Thursday night with the children. Also, once a month I had a date with Melody and once a month I had a date with Cindy. Those were wonderful times of sharing for all of us.

I found that the girls were much more relaxed talking to me about what was going on in their lives while we were shopping or eating out or going to the movies. If I had tried to force a fatherly conversation, it wouldn't have been the same. If I had said something like, "Well, let's sit down now. It's time to talk. So talk," I doubt if I would have gotten much response.

The Strong Silent Type

In the wake of the "women's movement," many men are erupting in anger. They feel their manhood has been compromised over the past two decades, and they're looking for change.

In its Fall 1990 special edition on the family, *Time* magazine reported that men are fed up with the bad rap the feminist movement has put on them. One man, a Washington, D.C., environmentalist, lashed out at feminists who "have been busy castrating American males." Another, described as a leader of the emerging "men's movement," says men are returning to the bedrock of their masculinity, throwing over the false dictates and anti-male sentiments of the 1960s and 1970s.

But men aren't the only ones fed up with male bashing. The article also reported that many women are apparently sick of the wimpy, limp-wristed creatures feminist logic created. They're tired of the Alan Alda image and want their men more in the mold of Mel Gibson and Arnold Schwarzenegger: what the writers call "the devoted family man with terrific triceps."

The fallout of this reexamination of values seems to be leading to a new definition of manhood, but in the men's own terms. One California broadcaster pointed out that no feminist would accept a man's definition of femininity; so why should any man accept a woman's definition of masculinity?

But the fact is, we are all defined by our roles and our relationships. A man is defined by his career, his marital status, his children, and his various activities and responsibilities. A woman, in turn, is defined by her career, her marital status, her children, and all of the things she has committed herself to being. Both are defined by their relationships to each other, and both are subject, ultimately, to God's definition of man, woman, and the family.

The Real Woman

Time magazine's poll of 505 men and women indicated that young women no longer believe that a career outside the home is the most important goal in life. One young woman, a second-year law student at Georgetown University, was quoted as saying, "We have a fear of being like the generation before us, which lost itself." Instead, these women seem to be learning that family and personal relationships take precedence over mere financial success. The same young woman also said, "I don't want to find myself at thirty-five with no family."

Workaholism is out; families are in. The *Time* poll reported that 51 percent of the respondents ranked having a long and happy marriage and raising well-adjusted children ahead of career success. Only 29 percent felt that career came first.

At the same time, nearly 75 percent of those surveyed felt that having a good marriage is more difficult today. More than half said they wanted their own marriage relationship to be different from that of their parents, but 85 percent felt their own generation is more likely to experience marital trouble and divorce than their parents' generation.

Young women surveyed tended to look on the women's movement with disdain. The name Gloria Steinem was an epithet to many, and most were suspicious of the movement that values career achievements more highly than building a happy home and family.

Other values were interesting as well. While only 19 percent of females and 41 percent of males rated "physical attractiveness" as an essential requirement for a spouse, 100 percent of the women and 97 percent of the men rated "faithfulness" as essential.

Genuine Differences

The *Time* magazine feature also reported that men and women experience life differently and think differently. Quoting Harvard researcher Carol Gilligan, *Time* observed that "the sense of relationship, the interconnectedness of people" is the central issue for most women. For women, relationships provide the equilibrium for life. "The terror for women," the article suggests, "is isolation."

The differences in attitudes between men and women can be seen in their core beliefs: that is, the things that make the difference between living and dying. One study from the mid-1970s showed that when men try to kill themselves, it is often because of injured pride or failures related to work. When women attempt suicide, however, it is usually because of a love relationship, a family failure, or a lost friend.

These studies reinforce the various images we have been developing, balancing the unique interrelatedness of women against the unique self-reliance and independence of most men.

The *Time* article says that relationships color every aspect of a woman's life. Women see conversation as a means of sharing and connecting with others; men tend to see conversation as a means of solving problems. Women believe in mutual dependence; men want freedom. Women see specific actions as elements of a long series of other actions; men see each event as specific and separate from others.

Gilligan's research also points out the differences in men's and women's attitudes about group activities. In men's sports, for example, an injured player is simply taken off the field and the game goes on. In women's games, when a teammate is injured, the game stops.

In justice, the Harvard study revealed that women are less concerned about abstract standards of right and wrong and more interested in finding compromises that maintain social balance. As an example of this finding, the writers cited Gilligan's 1982 book, *In a Different Voice* (Harvard University Press, 1982), in which she discusses a particular research example.

In the study, a boy and girl, both eleven, were asked whether a poor man would be doing the right thing to steal a drug that would save his wife's life. The boy said yes; human life is more valuable than mere property. The girl said no; he should borrow the money or work out payments with the druggist. The girl argued that if the husband went to jail, his wife would be in even worse circumstances, and he would be unable to help her.

Related studies showed that the differences in relating begin very early in boys and girls. Up until age three, both are very dependent upon their mothers. The mother-child relationship continues in little girls for several more years; however, by age four boys are already beginning to withdraw from their mother's care, seeking greater freedom and independence.

Beyond these findings, the Harvard researchers run into controversy, however, because they blame male-dominated society for the lack of self-esteem in women instead of looking more seriously into the broader issues of "socialization" in Western society. Nevertheless, their findings are enlightening.

Coming to Grips with Reality

The final and most important point is that we all have a vital need to return to the biblical concept that husbands and wives should *complete* each other, not *compete with* each other.

Scripture reminds us that God has given man to make woman whole, and woman to make man whole. I am not a complete person without my wife. I need Jan's insights, wisdom, and femininity to make me whole as a person. And she needs my insights, wisdom, and masculinity to make her whole as a person. That is why Scripture says it is not good for man or woman to be alone. We come together for wholeness. (Singles and God-ordained celibates also may come to wholeness—but that is a topic for another book.)

We must all see our spouses as God's *gift* to us. We should be completing each other, not competing with each other. And in order to do that, I suggest that we rediscover the biblical mandate for relating to other people.

Philippians 2:2-4, in a modern translation, reads:

> Live together in harmony, live together in love, as though you had only one mind and one spirit

between you. Never act from motives of rivalry or personal vanity, but in humility, think more of one another than you do of yourselves. None of you should think only of his own affairs, but should learn to see things from other people's points of view. (PHIL)

Someone has said that acceptance in marriage is the power to love someone and receive him or her in the very moment that we realize how far he or she falls short of our hopes. Acceptance in marriage is love between equals. It is love between two people who see clearly that they do not always measure up to each other's dreams. Acceptance is loving the real person to whom one is married. Acceptance is giving up dreams for reality. It seems to me that that is what a healthy marriage is really all about.

THREE

WHAT IS A HEALTHY MARRIAGE?

By now we should recognize that the marital bond is the most important relationship in any family. If the husband-wife relationship is healthy, then usually the parenting process will be healthy. But if it is unhealthy, then unhealthy traits usually will be acted out in all the other relationships in the family.

Researchers who have analyzed the development of the marital bond have found eight characteristics of healthy marriages. The same characteristics that make for healthy marriages make for healthy parenting. Since the husband-wife relationship is the cornerstone of the family, that will be our point of focus. Let's explore those eight traits.

Traits of a Healthy Marriage

The first trait of a healthy marriage is the *sense of individuation,* as opposed to enmeshment. That is, each partner knows who he or she is. One is not wrapped up in the other in an unhealthy way.

You have probably known women who get their entire identity from their husbands. As we saw in the first chapter, that is a type of enmeshment, and it is not healthy.

And you may know husbands who get their identity from their wives; that is also an unhealthy enmeshment.

There are also parents who get their whole sense of identity from their kids. If you don't believe it, go out some evening and watch a little league baseball game or a youth league soccer match. The identification with the kids is so great for some of these parents that if their child fails to do well, one or both parents can go straight down the tubes. Know what I mean? Believe me, that is unhealthy.

There must be a sense of separateness in the healthy family. Again, this is the idea behind the Scripture's admonition to "leave and cleave." Too many people get into unhealthy marriages because they don't divorce their parents before they marry their spouses. I always try to encourage people to make sure they've gotten divorced from their childhood relationships before they take on adult ones. There has to be a process of individuation, of pulling away from old dependencies.

As you can imagine, I see all sorts of difficulty in that process. Sometimes the kids try to pull apart, but the parents won't let them; that can be very painful and disruptive for parents and children alike. I am convinced that most in-law problems are generally caused by parents who won't quit parenting.

The second trait of a healthy family is *flexibility,* the ability to give and take, to go with the flow, and to keep a sense of humor. Whether it is in the way the husband and wife relate to each other, the way parents and children relate to each other, or in the way siblings relate to each other, flexibility is key. Flexibility helps to maintain a sense of balance and order in the family.

The third trait is *stability,* as opposed to uncertainty and disorganization. A sense of stability in the home helps to provide an atmosphere of structure and organization. That's where everybody knows the ground rules, and there is general agreement. Stability is the opposite of chaos.

Have you ever been in a home where things were out of control, chaotic? Maybe you've lived in one! It's where everyone is going in opposite directions all the time—no agreement, no cooperation, no common goals or plans. If it seems hysterical from the outside, just imagine what it must be like on the inside!

To be healthy and stable, there must be a sense of cohesion and unity in the family. There must be a sense that the family is united, that there are mutual goals and beliefs. So stability within the home is very important. The ability to cope with change and all the various demands that are put upon us each day (both adults and children) demands flexibility and stability.

The fourth trait is *clear perception,* as opposed to distorted perception, of who we are. Who am I? What is my role as a husband, a father, a son? What are my wife's duties as a wife, a mother, a daughter? If our perceptions are on track, we will perceive clearly who we are and how we relate to our children. We will also perceive clearly how we should relate to our parents. With balance in this area, we can recognize how our duties and responsibilities change as we move through the various stages of our lives.

It is interesting to observe that the way people perceive facts is often more important than the actual facts they perceive. It is also interesting to watch people trying to correct their perceptions of the facts. It almost never works. A lot of fad books have come along trying to do just that: trying to change perceptions without first helping people to make substantial changes to the inner being. But when we change only our perceptions, we just deal with how we *perceive* truth. If we want real inner change, we have to get down to truth itself.

At that point we move into God's territory. God alone knows what is true. We often think we do, but we always see things through our own set of filters, and there is always an element of distortion in our perceptions. Unless the channels of communication are open and there is clear agreement between a husband and wife, chances are their perception of how things are going in their marriage will actually be quite different.

When we have things in proper balance in the home and our thinking is seasoned by God's counsel, we can move along very well. But when things get out of balance, we lose perspective. This is generally the point at which someone like me can help. As a professional counselor, part of my job is to help provide a sense of objectivity and a clear perception of what's going on.

The fifth trait of the healthy marriage, arising directly from the preceding discussion, is *clear communication.* From what I have seen in family practice, I would estimate that 80 to 85 percent of marital difficulties are caused by communication difficulties and distorted communication. Consequently, I will want to talk about that later in more detail.

The sixth trait is *a sense of mutuality,* as opposed to isolation. I would suggest, for our purposes, that mutuality can be translated as intimacy. It is a sense of closeness and of "oneness" as opposed to a feeling of being cut off from the spouse or family. In healthy families there's a sense of mutuality, of sharing, of being open to one another, and of cooperation. When I see a family or a marriage where everybody is backing away and distancing themselves from the others, I know there are serious problems.

The seventh trait is *a sense of rapport* in the family. The French word *rapport* means an intense sense of unity and identity. It is a form of "support" that is, in fact, a unique kind of love. It's where each person recognizes and sustains the identity and value of the other person, or in our case, the other members of the family.

This sense of rapport also has to do with our roles in the family. People need to know what their roles are. It was during the 1960s and 1970s, when the unisex movement was all the rage, that American families really started to crumble. Men and women lost their sense of role. Successful relationships became hopeless in such a state.

I'm not promoting the stereotypes, but husbands and wives need to know their roles in their families. Equally important, both partners need to agree on those roles if they expect to have a healthy marriage. What you consider to be your role in your marriage may not be what I consider to be my role in my marriage. But it's important for you and your spouse to clearly understand your roles.

Lack of agreement, or unclear understanding of our roles, creates unhealthy marriages. And I think the blurring of sex roles has created incredible unhealthiness that borders on pathology in many so-called "modern marriages."

The eighth characteristic of a healthy family is *a clear sense of boundaries.* In a healthy relationship there are clear boundaries between the roles and responsibilities of each member; there is also a clear understanding of generational boundaries.

There must be distinctions between the roles of adults and children, but there also must be distinctions for husbands and wives. I know of marriages where the husband is primarily the father and the wife is the little girl. In others, the wife is the mother and the husband is more like a little boy. As you can imagine, potentially those are both pathological situations.

If the woman feels as though she has an extra child, her husband, inevitably there will be serious problems. And, if the husband feels as though he always has to take care of his little girl, who happens to be his wife, that will also lead to problems.

Relative Issues

Researchers have confirmed that the eight characteristics described above are the most common qualities of healthy families. If put into subgroups, there are four basic family issues, or themes. Let's examine them one at a time.

The *first* subgroup has to do with the identity process. That is *individuation versus enmeshment* and *mutuality versus isolation*. In families with healthy individuation and a sense of mutuality, individual family members know who they are and have a sense of their own identity. Family members have autonomy and know where boundary lines are. But they also know what they have chosen to share and risk together.

It is important that we each have our own identity. Some marriages get sick because the wife puts too many psychological eggs in her husband's basket. She depends upon him to give her all her good feelings about herself, and all her emotional support. Some husbands do the same thing with their wives. Those are what we call "identity problems."

The *second* subgroup of issues has to do with the ability to handle change. Anybody living in the twentieth century needs to have coping skills to deal with incredibly rapid change. If you have ever read any of the books such as *Future Shock* (Random House, 1970) or *The Dynamics of Change,* you know just what I mean. Regardless of how well-adjusted we may be, the pace of change is almost beyond our ability to cope with it.

The *third* set of basic family themes is what I call information processing. What do we hear from each other? How do we perceive? How is information shared? How is it received? How is it interchanged? Do we have open and clear communication with each other? If not, what are we doing to work on it and to improve it?

The *fourth* and final group deals with role structuring. Who are the parents and who are the children? Who is the father and who is the mother? Who is the husband, and who is the wife? Those are very important dynamics in a healthy family.

Confirming the Trends

One of this country's leading Christian magazines recently conducted a survey of their readership which included thousands of Christian families all over America. Readers were asked what they considered to be the key ingredients of a healthy marriage. The responses covered fifteen key elements that the editors then ranked by frequency of response. It's amazing how similar the magazine's list is to the eight characteristics listed above. Here's their entire list.

1. *Communication and listening.* You notice that those surveyed combined the two elements of conversation into one item. Communication certainly involves listening, but family members must

learn to both speak and listen clearly, and that is not always an easy combination.

2. *Affirmation and support.* I said earlier that people in healthy families will feel affirmed and supported by all members of the family. The magazine survey confirms that statement.

3. *Mutual respect.* The husband should respect the wife, the wife should respect the husband, and the parents should respect their children and teach them to respect the parents. This kind of respect will, of course, blossom in all our other relationships. An attitude of mutual respect inside the home will be reflected in a wholesome respect for others outside the home.

4. *A sense of trust.* The partners don't wonder if they can trust each other; it is understood. It's in the air they breathe. In turn, a healthy family carries a sense of trust among all its members.

5. *A sense of play and humor.* There needs to be a sense of humor in our families. If we can't keep our humor in the midst of marriage, we are in deep water, especially if we're raising kids. We need to learn to laugh at ourselves and to laugh with others.

6. *A sense of shared responsibility.* Nobody should feel as though he or she is carrying the whole load. And all family members should feel like they're important parts of the family.

7. *A sense of right and wrong.* This means that there is a natural and understood value system. Over the years, each family should have established firm boundaries so that everybody knows where he or she stands.

8. *A strong sense of family tradition.* These are the

activities that families do together and that they
will remember the rest of their lives. It may be
the way they celebrate Christmas or birthdays, or
visit grandparents in the fall. Maybe it's what
they do on vacation, the way they travel; or the
way they display trophies or awards or other
ornaments around the house. How many of your
family traditions and rituals do you remember?
Most of us remember these things with a sense of
joy and happiness. The magazine respondents
said they agreed that healthy families have a
strong sense of tradition and ritual.

9. *A balance of interaction among members.* No one member dominates the rest of the family. People feel
   they can contribute because they can share
   openly and equally.

10. *A shared religious core.* From a Christian perspective,
    that would mean the family has a shared com-
    mitment to Jesus Christ. When Mom and Dad
    are committed to Christ, the children will share
    and value that commitment. It won't necessarily
    solve all the problems, but there is a basic reli-
    gious value system and a basic commitment that
    provides a reliable and predictable foundation to
    everything else in the home.

11. *Respect for one another's privacy.* Everybody has a feel-
    ing that he has some corner of the house or
    room that is his own and exclusively his. To feel
    secure within the home, each person must feel
    that his privacy will not be violated by others.

12. *Valuing service to others.* I find that very interesting.
    Healthy families don't simply focus on their own
    happiness and welfare; they are also concerned
    for others, and they're involved in various kinds

of service. That is certainly in keeping with our
Lord's teaching. Jesus said that in losing yourself
you find yourself. So if you want to find yourself,
give yourself away. That is a very healthy trait.

13. *They share meals at the family table.* Historically, the
dinner hour was a time of family togetherness,
when everyone came and talked and shared
what was going on in their lives. It was a fun
time, a good time. Sadly, our society seems to be
moving away from this tradition. But these Christian families said it is still an important part of
the healthy home. I certainly agree.

14. *Family leisure activity on a regular basis.* Those surveyed believed that members of healthy families
have learned to share leisure time. They do leisure activities together, and they support and
encourage each other in these activities.

15. *Willingness of individuals to admit to their own problems and to seek help with them.* Underlying that
observation is, first, a fundamental belief that
one's trust will not be violated; second, that
others want to and are able to help; and third,
that no one will exploit a family member's admis-
sion of failure. Those are major assumptions, but
they are important for family security and unity.

The Roots of Behavior

All of us, in some way, are products of how we were
raised. However hard we may try, we can never totally
escape our upbringing. There are things from our childhood that will affect us the rest of our lives. One is where
we grew up; another is the parenting process under
which we grew up; and another is our biological heritage.
All of these things impact us.

One very interesting study traces the way parenting and heredity influence behavior. Perhaps a diagram will show it best. The vertical line represents the level of support in a family. At the top is a high support level and the bottom is low (or no) support.

LIMIT SETTING / NURTURING DIAGRAM

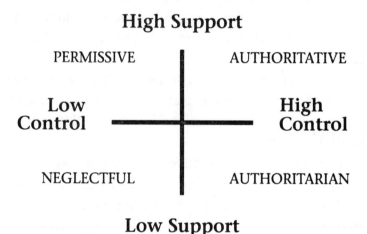

High Support

PERMISSIVE   AUTHORITATIVE

Low Control   **High Control**

NEGLECTFUL   AUTHORITARIAN

Low Support

The horizontal line represents parental control, going from a low level of control on the left to high control and dominance on the right. All of the creative tensions of growing up are represented somewhere within the four quadrants. Can you place yourself on this diagram?

As we were growing up, either we felt very little support from our parents, or we felt very high support from them. Either we felt there were very few rules, or we felt there were a lot of rules.

Now, as those two tensions come together, they create four quadrants, which represent all the basic parenting styles. For example, if you grew up in a home where there was high affirmation and support of you as a person but very few rules, you grew up in what we call a *permissive* home. If in your home there were very few rules and very little support of you as a person, you grew up in what we call a *neglectful* home.

If you were reared in a home where there was very little support of you as a person, but lots of rules, you had an *authoritarian* home. But if you grew up in a home where there was high support, high affirmation of your person-hood, but very clearly defined rules, then you had an *authoritative* home.

Now what are the results of these various types of parenting? Let me ask you to take a risk. Which of these four quadrants do you think tends to produce children with the highest self-esteem?

If you said the authoritative home, you answered correctly. The home where there is high support and high control provides security and rules that promote stability. In those kinds of homes, there are high expectations, but the children feel affirmed.

Now, which family do you think produces the lowest self-esteem? Answer: the neglectful home.

Next, which one of these homes do you think produces the children most likely to be drug- and chemical-abuse free? The authoritative home again.

Which do you believe would be the second most likely to be drug free? Believe it or not, the authoritarian home. "Dad will kill me" is not necessarily a bad fear if it keeps kids safe and responsible.

Which one of these types of homes tends to produce children who end up being the most productive in society? Again, the answer is the authoritative home.

The Nurturing Home

This upper right hand quadrant, which is a creative tension between clearly established ground rules and tremendous affirmation, is clearly a powerful and positive home environment. This combination tends to produce kids with high self-esteem, who are the least likely to get into drug and substance abuse, and also who tend to be the most productive.

Does this bring any verse of Scripture to mind? Change "support" to "nurture," and change "control" to "admonition" and see what you get. See if it brings any verse to mind. Ephesians 6:4 says, "Fathers, provoke not your children to wrath, but bring them up in the nurture and admonition of the Lord" (KJV).

Isn't that interesting? Two thousand years ago the Lord gave us the plan for raising healthy kids, but in a creative balance: nurture and admonition.

Usually we know how to admonish, but we don't always know how to nurture. Or perhaps we know how to nurture, but don't know how to admonish. If we can just learn to nurture and admonish, we will tend to raise healthy children and create healthy families. I find it fascinating that practical, empirical research simply confirms what God has already laid down for us in Scripture.

Self-esteem develops over our entire lives, from childhood on, but the roots are established in the nurturing home. If we have good feelings about who we are, and if those feelings are reinforced by others around us, we generally develop strong emotional health. But if we are convinced by everything we hear and see that we are of little value, then we are bound to suffer and to carry deep wounds around with us wherever we go.

The better we feel about ourselves, the more willing we are to take risks. But if we're down on ourselves, and feel like born losers, we are not as likely to open up and share ourselves with someone else. Obviously, low self-esteem will be a barrier to forming mature relationships, and it can become a chronic source of conflict in marriage.

Revealing Temperament

In a research project with couples who had recently been through marriage and premarital counseling, the Ministry Center staff at Highland Park Presbyterian Church compared results of the Taylor Johnson Temperament Analysis (TJTA) to a standard marital satisfaction inventory to determine the degree of marital satisfaction in the home.

We wanted to see if happy marriages could be predicted by examining the profiles of the TJTA. We had some hunches about it, but a lot of our hunches proved to be false. But we started to discover some fascinating correlations immediately. The first strong correlation we found was that in every marriage that showed a "high marital satisfaction" factor, both partners in the marriage also scored high on the self-esteem scale.

Technically, correlation does not prove causation, but in this case it suggests that when people who basically feel good about themselves get married, their chances of having good marital adjustment are considerably higher than they would be for people who do not feel good about themselves.

If you come into marriage feeling bad about yourself, you are likely to expend more energy on self-defense than on building the relationship. If you feel inferior, you are less likely to take emotional risks or to settle down peacefully with your mate. You are more likely to hold back, trying to protect yourself, so you won't get hurt anymore.

Low self-esteem is a jailer holding you captive, restraining you from the commitment and the happiness that comes with investing yourself and taking emotional risks. If you care about other people, you have to be careful with what you say. Words can be dangerous weapons if used carelessly. Even when people say things "for your own good," they can be destructive. Consequently, it is very hard for any of us to hear constructive criticism. You have to have a strong sense of self-worth to take criticism gracefully.

Somebody may say, "Well, I think you laid an egg, and I just wanted to tell you that whether you wanted to hear it or not." If you have any serious doubts about your worth as a person, such a comment can be crippling. Even if you have a healthy sense of self-esteem, it will sting. But you'll get over it and maybe learn something from it. Life is full of bumps and bruises; you have to be elastic to keep on going. If you're stiff and unyielding, you're going to be scarred by such experiences.

Guilt feelings also create barriers to intimacy in marriage. For example, it is almost impossible for people engaged in extramarital affairs to feel close to their spouses because the guilt they feel becomes a barrier. So they may try to cast the spouse as a monster in order to justify what they're doing.

Scripture says that the human heart is deceitful and desperately wicked (Jeremiah 17:9). When people defile their marriage vows through adultery, they can deceive even themselves. Then, instead of placing the guilt where it belongs, the adulterous spouse tries to pin the blame on his or her partner, the offended spouse. Obviously this can be a major barrier to closeness and intimacy.

Some people may feel guilty about certain thoughts, dreams, or other fantasies. A husband may think, "My wife would think I'm weird if she knew what I was thinking." A wife may be afraid her husband would put her away if he knew the things that went through her mind. Guilt feelings can take control of their lives.

Under such a cloud, these individuals are not likely to take emotional risks, and that places the health of the marriage relationship at risk. Clearly, cleansing the heart and conscience is God's work, so he needs to be part of the healing process.

Setting Priorities

Still another serious threat to a healthy marriage—especially for the families I minister to in the Highland Park area of Dallas—is chronic busyness!

Do you ever feel like you're in a rat race? Do you ever feel that you're so busy you want to stop the bus and walk? How do you two manage to find time for each other if you're that busy? For many couples, it's impossible. They just don't have time.

Some young couples who come to see me complain about all the problems in their marriages. When I look at their calendars, it's like looking at an airline schedule. They're booked up all day everyday, and not with each other!

They say, "We don't feel close." So I ask them, rather bluntly, "Have you ever stopped to see how little time you spend with each other? Nobody could feel close with the kind of schedules you two have!"

One couple had a similar complaint. In addition to their jobs and a variety of civic and social commitments, they had three sons, and each son was in two soccer leagues. Between practice and games and all the other activities in their lives, there wasn't enough time in the week. So I said to them, "You people are insane. How can you survive like this?" They got the message and decided to eliminate some of that stuff.

That's just busyness. Some people get busy to avoid intimacy. For one man I counseled, just the idea of intimacy was terribly frightening, so he poured himself completely into his work. He knew that otherwise, he would have to go home and relate to his wife and family. Needless to say, he had a serious problem that needed time and healing. Once we identified the real problem, however, he was willing to work on it.

I find that some women do much the same thing with committees, clubs, or church work. That's *their* busyness. Whenever the husband comes home, there's no time to relate because the wife's at church, or at a committee meeting, or whatever. That is not a healthy situation.

Does that mean she shouldn't be involved in the church or other organizations? No. But if she is using the church or the Junior League or a bunch of committees just to stay busy and out of touch, then it is wrong and she should stop.

Remember, God created the family as the first institution. If God considered the home to be the first and most important organization in his creation, then we should too!

At one time, Jan and I came to a place in our lives where we were going to so many Christian meetings that we didn't have time to be Christian. So we gave up some of our Christian activities for Lent.

You talk about going through guilt—just quit doing some of your Christian busywork and check out your guilt gauge. A lot of us have equated being committed to committees as the same as being committed to the Lord.

I'll never forget when I first decided I was going to quit some of those Christian meetings and that I was going to stay home and be more Christian, spending time with my family. That was a major step for me, and at the time, I wasn't very sure that I was doing the right thing. I had grave doubts, but I knew I had to make some changes. Today I see that as one of the best decisions I ever made and one of the greatest steps I have ever taken for my own sanity.

Today I will never commit to more than one civic responsibility a year because I have decided that taking on more than that is to surrender time that rightfully belongs to my family and to me. It is a crime to take on time-consuming projects for the sake of busyness, and to deprive myself and my family of time we should be spending together.

I know some people who are on every conceivable board of directors. I suspect that kind of "joiner" is probably more on an ego trip than trying to help. I know both men and women who get trapped by the same nonsense. They wonder why they don't have time for their families.

If you want to have a close relationship with God, you need time with him. If you want to have a close relationship with your spouse, you need time with him or her. There is no substitute for spending time with the one you love.

Quantity versus Quality

You have heard some people say it's not the quantity of time but the quality of time. That is pure nonsense. That line is an excuse invented by people who simply refuse to spend time with their loved ones. You cannot condense a world of quality into thirty seconds. When you sell out your loved ones for busyness, you do them and yourself a great disservice.

I am reminded of C. S. Lewis's well-known example of

the man who went into a restaurant and ordered a steak. When the waiter returned, he brought out the finest steak money could buy, wonderfully seasoned and piping hot, but exactly one-inch square. Quite understandably, the customer was very upset; he had wanted a whole steak, not just a bite.

But the waiter protested. "Sir, I assure you that this is the finest steak money can buy. You won't find a better cut anywhere in the world. The quantity may not be much, but the quality is superb, and everybody knows it's the quality that counts, not the quantity!"

Do you think the customer would be satisfied with that logic? Of course not. Your children and your spouse should not be, either. Lewis went on to argue that there is no quality without quantity, especially in human relationships. I agree.

Dealing with Anger

Misplaced anger can also create a threat to marital health. In other words, the way we handle our anger with each other has a lot to do with how we communicate. If we resort to hostility, we wound our loved ones, and we destroy communication. But if we do the opposite and just suppress our anger, it will tend to come out in other ways. For example, we may begin sniping and picking at each other. Have you ever felt that going on? Pick, pick, pick, pick. Irritating isn't it?

That kind of sniping and picking means that we are actually suppressing or swallowing our major source of anger. It's like trying to hold a beach ball under water. You can hold it down and sit on it for a while, but sooner or later, it will pop up somewhere.

That is why the Scripture directs us to deal with anger. Paul wrote, "'Be angry, and do not sin' do not let the sun go down on your wrath" (Ephesians 4:26), and "Put away from you . . . all malice" (4:31). Malice is anger being worked out destructively.

Dealing with anger is discussed in more detail in chapter 5.

A Healthy Marriage Is Possible

Recognizing the patterns of a healthy marriage is what we've been working on in this chapter. All of us have basic human needs, and if we're not getting at least some of those needs met constructively, in a caring and loving environment, we will be in trouble.

As we saw earlier, the Scripture calls for the wife to be sensitive to her husband's needs and for the husband to be sensitive to his wife's needs. There has to be some reciprocal give and take in a healthy marriage.

If both the husband and wife will follow that biblical model and try to be sensitive to each other's needs, then, believe it or not, both of their needs will be met. But if there is "mutual need deprivation," then they will have real barriers to intimacy. They will be so needy that there won't be enough left to risk.

Someone has written: "Above all other things in marriage, enhance your spouse's self-esteem." That is marvelous advice. In fact, that would probably transform most marriages if couples would do it.

FOUR

THE AWESOME POWER OF THE LISTENING EAR

In the previous chapters we explored some of the different types of marriages and saw that a happy family is one where there is mutual respect, affirmation, and support. The key passage was Genesis 2:24: "Therefore shall a man leave his father and his mother, and shall cleave unto his wife: and they shall be one flesh" (KJV).

Another passage offers additional keys to what is perhaps the single most important element of a healthy marriage—a healthy communication process. James 1:19 says, "Let every man be swift to hear, [and] slow to speak." My guess is that most people live by another rule, which says, "Let everybody be quick to speak and slow to hear."

I would like to suggest that every healthy marriage has, as one of its most important ingredients, an atmosphere in which both partners believe they are heard and listened to fairly.

I have dealt with many unhappy marriages where there was not a level of open and equal communication, but I have never dealt with a healthy marriage where that kind of open communication was missing. In marriages where both husband and wife feel that the other partner is at least listening to them, there is always hope for reconciliation.

Usually, I like to talk to men and women about open communication very early in our discussions. I start by talking about learning to articulate our needs and feelings successfully. For the purposes of this book, however, I would like to start by focusing on the most challenging part first: that is, learning how to listen carefully. In my life, listening is much more difficult than talking. I find that most couples have the same experience.

A Listening Checkup

One of the first things I do in a group setting is to ask the couples to take a listening skills test. You may want to try this yourself. If so, you will need a piece of paper on which to write your answers, but you will have to listen with your eyes.

The story goes like this:

A businessman had just turned off the lights in the store when a man appeared and demanded money. The owner opened the cash register. The contents of the cash register were scooped up and the man sped away. A member of the police force was notified immediately.

Now, what follows is a true-false test. As you go down the list of questions, write your responses on a slip of paper: True or False.

1. A man appeared after the owner had turned off his store lights.
2. The robber was a man.
3. The man did not demand money.
4. The man who opened the cash register was the owner.
5. The store owner scooped up the contents of the register and ran away.
6. Someone opened the cash register.
7. After the man who had demanded money scooped up the contents of the cash register, he ran away.
8. While the cash register contained money, the story does not state how much.
9. The robber demanded money of the owner.
10. Only three persons are referred to: the owner of the store, a man who demanded money, and a member of the police force.

At this point, we review our responses to see if we agree on what we heard. We all agree, at least, that we heard the same story.

I find that the responses usually come as follows:

1. About half will say "True" and half "False."
2. Also half and half.
3. Generally, about a third say "True."
4. About half and half.
5. Most will say "False," but a few say "True."
6. About two-thirds generally say "True."
7. Usually, between a fourth and half say "True."
8. About half and half.
9. About two-thirds normally say "False."
10. Generally between 40 and 50 percent say "True."

Then comes the fun part. It's always fun to observe that in every group of people, whether it's a large group or small one, and even though everybody has heard the same story, there is enormous disagreement over what they heard!

The reason is simple. This is a very ambiguous story. The problem is that whenever we don't get enough information, we tend to fill in the blanks with our own presuppositions, our own personal biases, and our own assumptions. You will see what I mean as I go back over the story.

The fact is, only one of the statements should have been answered true based on the information given: number six. Consider the first statement, the answer to which is false: a man appeared after the owner turned off the lights. The story says that a businessman turned off the lights in the store when a man appeared and demanded money. It didn't say the businessman was the owner. Still, most people assume that the businessman and the owner are the same person. The owner could have been a woman. Because we don't have enough information, we fill in the blanks and make assumptions.

For statement two, was the robber a man? In the first place, there's no line in the story that says a robbery took place. It just says a man appeared and demanded money. This could have been the owner of the building, collecting rent. It could have been the owner's son or a friend, or somebody from the utility company. But because a member of the police force was notified, we assume a robbery took place. Again, we don't have enough information, so what do we do? We fill in the blanks.

Now don't worry if you let your imagination run away with you. The first time I took this test, I was with a group of two hundred counselors who were supposed to be highly skilled listeners. We did exactly what anybody else would do. We just went right down the middle in what we thought we heard. Half answered true for most of the questions, while the other half answered false.

The point is, we bring about 75 percent of what we hear to the listening process. In marriage, it is crucial to understand that fact. So often, what we hear from others are our own assumptions, our own presuppositions, that may or may not bear any resemblance to what was really said.

If You Could Read My Mind

One of the greatest mistakes that couples in unhealthy marriages make, over and over, is expecting the partner to read his or her mind. It is as if the person is saying, "You know what I mean. You have been with me long enough to know what I had in mind." But, obviously, we are not mind readers. If we were, there wouldn't be so many disputes in marriage. There would be little for marriage counselors to do.

In previous chapters, we talked about the differences between men and women. We saw that, generally speaking, men talk in generalities while women tend to talk in details. Women tend to *feel* first and *think* second. With men, it's the other way around.

Those are facts—not put-downs. They are not even matters of opinion. But while those facts are generally true, and have always been true, they continue to foul up the listening process. Often a woman will be listening for a man's feelings while he's telling her what he is thinking. Or a man will be listening for a woman's thoughts while she's describing what she is feeling.

Getting beyond such communication barriers to the place where we can really hear each other can be tricky business. This is why James wrote, "Let every man be swift to hear, [and] slow to speak" (James 1:19).

Somebody has said the Lord gave us two ears and one mouth, so we should listen twice as much as we speak. But maybe you have found, as I have, that any time your spouse is laying out the charges in even the most casual household dispute, you're already working on your defense speech before he or she is finished talking. Have you ever been in that situation? It's easy to feel threatened; and it's hard to hear what the other person is trying to say.

This is why people go to third parties that we call counselors who don't bring the same emotional baggage to the listening process. Counselors have the advantage of a simpler, more objective, listening environment.

It is fascinating for me as a marriage counselor to listen to what couples say to each other. I find myself trying to hear what they hear. Since I am not hearing with the same set of "filters," sometimes I have to guess what certain words mean to the warring couple. In some cases, couples have developed a personal jargon of "war words" that only they can understand. Without knowing their language, the counselor cannot understand all the presuppositions and assumptions.

Even in the best situations, listening is a very difficult art. And the fact that marriages are composed of two opposite sex people just complicates the matter unbelievably!

Through all of this, there is one other very important piece of information that you need to know. Whether it is in business, in a family, with friends, or in any other relationship, people need to feel good about themselves. One of the things my wife, Jan, and I should know about each other—and you should know about your spouse—is that all people need to feel good about themselves.

I did not get up this morning, look in the mirror and say, "I wonder what I can do today to feel really inadequate?" I doubt if you did either. If you did, drop me a letter and we'll set up a counseling appointment!

No, I need to feel good about myself. I want to feel good about who I am. I want to feel that I'm a decent father, a decent husband, a decent person. The degree to which you threaten that need makes it difficult for me to hear you.

The Defense Reaction

If Jan says to me, "Jim, I'd like to talk to you," and I suspect that she's going to attack me and criticize me, then my defenses will go up immediately. I may or may not want to talk to her, but I naturally assume a defensive posture.

This defense reaction is one of the reasons I believe there is hardly ever any such thing as constructive criticism. It takes an incredibly mature person to deal with constructive criticism. We have to be enormously secure in ourselves to be able to hear it without getting defensive.

Most of us go on the defensive immediately. Then, as soon as we're on our guard, we start preparing to take the offensive. We prepare for attack.

If I'm going to participate in a give-and-take dialogue, I need to feel good about myself. But if I feel you've threatened that, there will be a barrier between us. That's why, in healthy marriages, both husband and wife need to learn skills that allow them to talk to each other about what's going on inside.

If we can find a way of discussing what we like and don't like about each other in a way that doesn't threaten the other person's sense of worth, then we will give each other the best chance of hearing what we have to say.

As a listener, my task is to be *swift to hear and slow to speak*. But that is not a natural instinct. It is an acquired behavior.

How do you like talking to your spouse when he or she just keeps interrupting you, finishing your sentences for you, or jumping ahead of you? It's as if he or she is saying, "Okay, I know where you're going with that. Now, let me tell you how the cow ate the cabbage!"

In a healthy marriage, we must learn to hear the other person out. The ability to set aside our own fears and biases takes a lot of skill—and a lot of prayer—because we naturally want to defend ourselves whenever we feel attacked. And, of course, that is equally true for both men and women.

Aiming for Understanding

What healthy marriages have that unhealthy marriages don't have is the ability to communicate openly and freely. If you learn only one thing from this book, I hope it will be this: the number one goal of communication in marriage is understanding, not agreement.

Let me repeat myself. *The number one goal of communication in marriage is understanding, not agreement.* If you insist on agreement, then you're into a form of communication called "persuasion." That ought to be made clear right up front.

I can try to hear what my wife is saying as long as I don't feel that she's going to insist that I agree with her. Knowing that Jan respects my rights gives me a better chance of actually hearing what she's trying to tell me— to hear the feminine viewpoint, or to hear her particular perspective—without having to make a judgment about whether she's right or wrong. I can just *hear* her. That is a very important ingredient in healthy marriages.

Even in a good marriage, there are strong defense mechanisms. If I feel that you will be going for my jugular, my instinct is to go for your jugular first. You don't have to be married very long to know how to get to your spouse's jugular!

Somebody has said that marriage is one long experiment in learning what you cannot talk about. In all marriages, there are certain buzz words guaranteed to start a fight.

Used with appropriate malice, those words are certain to send your spouse right into orbit. We learn how to push the buttons very quickly!

It's a tremendous temptation to go for one of those buttons, particularly if we are losing an argument. But in healthy marriages we have to learn (with God's help) how to hear the other person out, regardless of how threatened we may feel.

Dealing with Emotional Threats

It is important to understand how to deal with threats, because this issue causes many extramarital affairs. Have you ever thought that it might be easier to disclose something about yourself to a total stranger than to somebody very close to you?

If I tell Jan something deep about my feelings, such as a great fear or a deep feeling I may have, I give her one of two things. I hand her either an awesome weapon that she can use against me if she chooses, or an awesome tool that she can use to nurture me. I take that risk whenever I disclose my real feelings.

For example, suppose I told you, "I'm really very sensitive about not having much hair." If you saw me at a conference somewhere, you could say, "How's it going, Slick?" Because you knew that I was especially sensitive about my hair, you may have felt that you had some emotional advantage over me. By self-disclosing, I gave you something to gig me with—if you chose to use it. Now if you did not choose to gig me with it, then you would be very cautious about what you say about hair, especially mine, when I'm around. And you could use this self-disclosure as a nurturing tool. Either way, the private knowledge that I gave you becomes a sensitive area.

One thing that often happens when men and women talk to each other is that they discover how risky self-disclosure is. Later, in chapter 6, I will talk about the relationship between the degree of self-disclosure in a marriage and the amount of intimacy that is experienced—there is a connection. While it is true that self-disclosure in marriage or any other situation can be extremely risky, we should recognize that there are different levels of self-disclosure. In other words, what I disclose to you is one thing; what I disclose to my spouse may be something very different.

Let's say that after a particularly hard day at the office, I sit down by you and say, "Boy, I'm fed up with my job. Counseling is such a drag. I think I've had it up to here. Frankly, at lunchtime today I'd like to get in my car, go home, sell the house, fly to the Bahamas, rent a boat, and sail the islands until the money runs out."

That is really not an uncommon remark. We all have moments of fantasy like that. And my guess is that you would probably admit, "I can identify with that. There are times I've felt the same way."

But suppose I go home and say the same things to Jan? How would she respond? My candid self-disclosure might be a little more scary to her. Why? Because we're married.

There's a lot more to lose. There are a lot more ramifications. So sometimes our self-disclosures may be incredibly threatening to our spouse. As a result, we may start hiding our private emotions from one another.

This brings me to the most important of all listening skills: hearing what your spouse is saying without sucking air and falling off your chair. Or without getting out your prayer list!

I've always felt that a true Christian friend is somebody you can think out loud around without worrying about going to the top of his or her prayer list. So how do I do that around my spouse? How do I learn to handle scary information?

Opening Up

Part of listening well is responding in such a way that will encourage more self-disclosure rather than less. To be a true friend is to be open to the most personal emotions of those we care about without judging or condemning them.

Here's an example of what I mean. Let's take a fairly normal situation. The wife is a homemaker and the husband is in business for himself. He comes home at 6:00. When she takes one look at his face, she knows it has not been a good day.

She says, "Honey, what's wrong? Tell me about it." Now the wife wants what? Detail.

So he says, "I had a bad day."

And the wife says, "I know that, honey. Tell me about it." She wants to know what's bothering him—in detail.

So the husband decides, *Okay, I'll risk it.* "Well, we hired this secretary today. You wouldn't believe her. She can't spell; she can't file; she can't type; she can't handle the phone; she isn't attractive. She's just horrible."

That's a risky thing for a man to share with his wife because it involves a form of self-disclosure. He told her details about his work that she can use either as a bond or as a weapon.

Now what do you think the average wife would say to such a statement? "Why in the world did you hire her in the first place?" Or even more direct, "Why don't you just fire her?"

On a scale of one to ten, that's about a minus eleven. What her husband hears is, "Well, you dummy, anybody with a lick of sense knows how you solve that problem. You simply admit that you made a mistake and fire her. Sit down here, little boy, and I'll show you how to run your business."

So the husband makes a mental note, *That's the last time I share details with her. I didn't come home to be treated like a child.*

Suddenly they have lost contact. The line goes dead. Communication has ended. The wife only wanted to share with her husband, but the signals from both sides got mixed up and, in fact, the communication failed. Male-female signals have such a difficult time getting through.

So, what would be a healthy statement for the wife who wanted to encourage her husband to speak his mind? She might have said, "Oh, that's too bad. What can you do about it?" First, an expression of concern; second, respect for his right to decide. It is important how she responds.

She might even invite him to talk more about it, to tell how the secretary got hired in the first place and why he thinks that she's performing so badly.

She can use words of recognition and affirmation, such

as "I'm sure that's disappointing to you." Recognition and affirmation encourage further communication.

If we don't learn to deal with these subtleties, we will halt the whole communication process. The flow stops because one person feels put down. All the husband wants is empathy. He wants some understanding that he has a mess on his hands at the office.

Now he may or may not have much more to say about the situation at the office, but the way his wife handles that information either encourages more communication or chops it off.

Keeping the Channels Open

The same dynamics exist in parenting, and we have to learn to use some of the same processes of listening and affirmation with our children. If we're not careful, we can fall into the trap of being good parents instead of responsible parents.

What's the difference? Good parents always step in and rescue their kids. When parents constantly take command and take the responsibility for their children's decisions, the message communicated is that the kids can't handle it.

"Let Mother save you," they say in effect, or "Let Father rescue you." They don't mean it to come across that way, but that's often what the children hear.

Suppose the husband comes home and shares something with his wife about his work that is highly threatening to her. Maybe he comes home and says, "Honey, business is so bad, we may go under." Or, "I really pulled a royal screw-up today, and it's possible I will lose my job."

What would be a good response on the wife's part? She could say, "We'll work it out, dear." Another would be,

"I'm sorry, dear, but we'll see it through, together. I stand by you." That's very supportive.

What else might a person say in a healthy marriage? "I know you're hurting, and I'm hurting with you." That's affirming.

Does that make sense? Isn't that better than saying, "Well, how could you do something so stupid?" or any of a dozen such things. The idea is to listen first, to express support.

That is not an easy response to learn. I've got to be in touch with my own desires and feelings to maintain control. Now the wife certainly has the right to say, "That's very frightening to me." That would be honest communication. But statements like "We'll see it through together," "Thank you for sharing it with me," or "Thank you for risking it with me" build the bonds between husband and wife.

Isn't that really the most important thing you can do? Jobs come and go; there will be many problems during the course of your marriage; there will be failures and successes, one after the other, the rest of your life. But your marriage relationship and the bond between you is a lifetime commitment.

Developing a Listening Stance

Change is never easy, but it is inevitable. So your task in marriage is to nourish and cherish the partner with whom you plan to spend the rest of your life. Husbands must cherish and affirm their wives; wives must support and encourage their husbands. That's what it's really all about. And if that is not your personal goal, then I question your values.

The most important question you can ask yourself while listening to another person's intimate self-disclosure is, *What does this person want me to do with this information?*

Your response to that question will determine your listening stance. I always try to ask myself that question when people start opening up to me as a counselor.

Sometimes all people want is a sympathetic listener. We all endure a variety of hurts and pains, and we need to disclose our emotions. And many people need to talk to a professional who can help them digest their problems.

In my practice, sometimes people come in and for fifty minutes they just spill out their pain, hurt, and anger. And sometimes for those fifty minutes I just sit and say, "Hmmm. Is that right? Really? Gee. Really? Is that right?" To be sensitive and responsive, I need to let this person open up and reveal those issues and concerns. I need to adopt a "listening stance."

My listening posture in this situation is what I would call the "hold the bucket" stance. This is for people who just need to get out all their hurt, frustration, pain, anger, and disappointment. They aren't asking me to fix it— only to listen. I believe this is part of what Paul was suggesting in Galatians 6:2 when he wrote, "Bear one another's burdens, and so fulfill the law of Christ."

It is helpful to recognize that there is a layering process in life where attitudes and feelings are laid down one on top of another from childhood on. We begin to lean in one direction or another as we mature, based on the way our stacks take shape. And we all take on certain behavioral characteristics from the way attitudes and feelings are combined in our lives.

It is important to understand that all these layers are laid down by words, not by hypothetical or imaginary things, but by all the words we have heard or overheard in a lifetime. Positive and negative words all blend together, and our emotional responses give distinctive shape to our character and emotions.

In another sense, we are like computers, programmed with negative and positive symbols. If the negative information outweighs the positive, there will be a dangerous imbalance, and the whole structure may collapse. That's when we start looking at serious therapy, sorting through the pieces to understand why it all came apart.

Wouldn't it be nice if we could simply analyze the input as we are receiving it and separate the good stuff from the bad? Obviously there will be a lot of input we cannot control. But Scripture offers many ways of putting balance into our lives, and it helps us to sort through the debris. I want to explore some of those Bible passages, but first I think it will be helpful to see how this verbal layering takes place by listing eight basic steps in the verbal communication process.

The Imaginary and the Real

Every communication begins with an idea or a thought, something someone wants to express. Step one is *what I intend to say to you*. But, step two, which is the flip side, is *what I actually say.*

Have you ever discovered that in the process of speaking to someone, you inadvertently said something you didn't mean to or didn't want to say? Have you ever said something that didn't come out the way you intended? So that's what steps one and two are about: that is, what I apparently said to you as opposed to what I wanted to say.

Step three is *what you heard as opposed to what I said.* I have a sign in my office that expresses this kind of misunderstanding. It says, "I know you think you understand what I said; but what you don't understand is that what you heard is not what I meant!" Regardless of what I meant to say, you may have heard something entirely different than what I intended for you to hear.

Step four is *what you say to yourself about what you just heard.* You know, we are constantly talking to ourselves about our experiences. So when you see or hear something, such as my comment to you, you react internally first and externally only after you have digested that comment.

Step five is *what you intend to say back to me* in light of what you think you heard me say. Step six is *what you actually say*—or perhaps we should say, what you *communicate* to me—as opposed to what you intended to say.

Step seven is *what I hear as opposed to what you said;* and step eight is *how I talk to myself about what I think I heard you say* in response to what you thought you heard me say. We can mess it up in any one of those eight places.

Add to that the differences between our natural perceptions as men and women, and you can begin to understand why communication in marriage is so difficult. With all the other things going on in verbal and nonverbal communication, we should not be surprised to realize that there is a very complex range of interactions taking place.

Even the eternal God who made us has trouble communicating with us. Did you ever stop to think about that? The writer of Hebrews wrote, "God, who at various times and in different ways spoke in time past to the fathers by the prophets, has in these last days spoken to us by His Son" (Hebrews 1:1-2). Why did God speak through Christ? Because even after the people heard all the things the prophets said, they still didn't get it.

The Gospel of John tells us that God sent his Son, the Word, to dwell among us: "And the Word became flesh and dwelt among us, and we beheld His glory" (John 1:14).

Then, echoing the words of the prophet Isaiah, Jesus said that he chose to speak to the people in parables because they would not understand his words: "Therefore I speak to them in parables, because seeing they do not see, and hearing they do not hear, nor do they understand" (Matthew 13:13). Again and again God told people about his nature, but they did not get the message.

"In the beginning was the Word" (John 1:1) and "the Word became flesh" (John 1:14) are statements that Jesus Christ became a flesh-and-blood human being so that he could give us more evidence, verbal and nonverbal, of the nature of God. Even though the Son of God was crucified, his message, brought both by his words and his witness, changed the course of history. Nothing has been the same since that time.

My point is fairly simple. If God himself had such difficulty communicating with us, for whatever reasons, is it any wonder that we have trouble communicating with each other and hearing each other accurately?

Turning Away Wrath

The verbal process would be very difficult even if there were no other complications. But I want you to think about the verse we discussed earlier: James 1:19. Remember it? It says, "Let every man be swift to hear, slow to speak." That is the key to listening.

So what is the key to speaking? Two verses should be considered—one in the Old Testament and one in the New. The first is Proverbs 15:1. I'm sure you know it: "A soft answer turns away wrath, but a harsh word stirs up anger."

Paul underlined this concept in the second letter to

Timothy when he wrote, "A servant of the Lord must not quarrel but be gentle to all" (2 Timothy 2:24). In another place, Paul admonished Christians to be "speaking the truth in love" (Ephesians 4:15). And later he wrote, "Let all bitterness, wrath, anger, clamor, and evil speaking be put away from you, with all malice. And be kind to one another, tenderhearted, forgiving one another, just as God in Christ also forgave you" (Ephesians 4:31-32).

In healthy marriages, couples "speak the truth in love" and "forgive one another."

Do you realize you can speak the truth and not speak it in love? I've seen people level each other with the truth. When the other person is sitting in a heap, wiped out, then the person who has done the damage usually says something like, "You just can't stand the truth." How observant! You can kill somebody with the truth if you decide to use it as a weapon.

The book of Ephesians—an excellent book to read for insight into relationships—provides a lot of instruction in such matters. Ephesians 4 slides right into Ephesians 5 and 6, which are two of the great passages about family living in Scripture. These verses tell us that we need to learn to speak the truth in love to each other whether it is in the Body of Christ (the church), or in the body we call the family, the home.

What in the world is meant by "a soft answer" turning away wrath and speaking "the truth in love"? Many years ago, as a young Christian, I read the verse, "A soft answer turns away wrath." I thought it meant that whenever you got in a discussion you should lower your voice and speak very quietly; that would stop people from getting angry.

I soon discovered that it's not the volume that makes the difference. Have you ever been around somebody who would speak very softly through clinched teeth? I think that can be even more menacing than just yelling at someone. You are getting a nonverbal override. The nonverbal, clinched-teeth routine is telling you that, "I am really ticked at you!" Obviously that's not what the writer of Proverbs meant by "a soft answer."

Let me suggest to you that "a soft answer" means that, when I do speak, I have a Christian responsibility to think in terms of how what I'm going to say is going to land on you. I need to be sensitive to your emotions. Is what I have to say going to hit you hard? Is it going to hit you soft?

What did we say was one of the problems with listening? If I think you're going to attack me, where is my energy going to go? To defense. So if I don't want you spending all your energy defending yourself, working on your defense speech, then I'd better try to learn the skill of answering you softly. In other words, I need to think in terms of how my response to you is going to land on you.

When I speak what I perceive to be the truth to you, I need to learn to do it in love, and you need to feel that love. Otherwise, your energy will go to defense. This is not only true in marriage and in parenting, it's also true in work relationships. I think this is the truth implied in Ephesians 4:15 where it says, "speaking the truth in love."

The Problem, Not the Person

In psychological terms, one of the key principles of constructive communication is that "I" messages are safer than "you" messages. In fact, I would like to suggest another cardinal rule. Never use the word "you" unless it is followed by a compliment.

I'll even expand that: never use the word "never," and never use the word "always" unless they are followed by a compliment. If you perceive that someone behaves in a certain disagreeable way all the time, modify your statement. Say "sometimes."

If you say, "You're never on time," and he can recall at least once when he was punctual, he will quickly remind you of that time. "You always forget your tie." "You always forget your teeth." Unfortunately, we make such challenges almost routinely.

But those kinds of messages tend to create bigger fights and nastier hurts. They do not tend to improve communication between people. Does that seem like a reasonable rule? *Don't use "you" unless you follow it with a compliment; and never use "never" or "always" unless they're followed by a compliment.*

From my own experience I can tell you that's a tough rule to live by; so you may need to memorize it. Memorize it and rehearse it so it becomes a part of your life.

Safe Talk

Feelings statements like these are usually very safe: "I've got a problem." "I'm hurting." "I'm angry." "I'm frustrated." "I'm feeling inadequate." "I'm feeling rejected." "I'm feeling unneeded." "I'm feeling treated like a child."

The truth is that no one can argue with your feelings. They're not up for discussion. You feel what you feel. Of course, your spouse may wish you didn't feel that way. She or he may wish you felt differently. She or he may even hope you'll feel differently. But the point is, only you know what you're feeling.

If I tell Jan that she is insensitive, she will perceive that as an attack. "Janet, you're being insensitive." Honestly, I don't know if she feels like she's being insensitive or not. She may feel like she's working overtime at being sensitive. What I do know, though, is that I'm feeling unappreciated. I'm feeling neglected.

Jan cannot argue with that. She may wish it were different, but she cannot debate what I say I am feeling. The added advantage, especially in a dialogue of this type with a woman, is that women are generally attuned to feelings. We observed earlier that men, by and large, tend to respond to cold logic, but women will understand the importance of feelings.

Feelings statements are always safer than "you" statements, and they tend to promote constructive communication, not cut it off. I do not give a guarantee on this, but I will say that you have a much better chance of finding a peaceful solution by focusing back on yourself rather than on the other person.

I have a better chance of reaching an understanding with Jan if I say, "Honey, I'm feeling neglected; I'm feeling unappreciated; I'm feeling unloved," than if I say, "You don't appreciate me! You hate me!"

The only problem is that it's hard for most men to get in touch with what they're feeling. They're geared to the practical and the mundane, so it's natural for them to respond on a surface level. But they can learn to consider feelings first; anybody can. Getting in touch with feelings and emotions and with the more complex messages we transmit to each other is the subject of the next chapter.

FIVE

I Heard What You Didn't Say!

Is it possible to pay someone a compliment without words? Certainly. A smile is one way. Usually we interpret a smile as warm and friendly, as a sort of compliment. Touching is another way. A pat on the back or a friendly hug can be a powerful form of communication, if it's sincere.

One of the most interesting Bible studies I ever attended was a survey of the touching ministry of Jesus. In the course, we studied the people Jesus touched, where he touched them, why he touched them, and what happened. It was fascinating.

Jesus touched some people you weren't supposed to touch in those days: lepers, tax collectors, blind and lame people, and harlots. Why do you suppose he did that?

Jesus said, "I have come that they may have life, and that they may have it more abundantly" (John 10:10). Do you suppose Christ's touch was an expression of his life-giving power? Clearly it gave life to Jairus's daughter, whom he raised from the dead by his touch. I think it is fair to say that life comes to anyone touched by Christ.

For many years now, important clinical research has

demonstrated that touching is a very real part of our human needs. In fact, we know that children who are raised without experiencing touching and without being held may actually die. This is especially true in institutions where children have been raised in rather cold and austere surroundings without much physical contact or personal nurturing.

Touching is a powerful form of communication that doesn't involve words. Sometimes, after an argument, you and your spouse may both be tired of fighting, but you would really prefer for your mate to crawl back to you instead of you to your mate. Right?

So later that night when you're lying in bed, one of you reaches out and touches the other person. That says so much, doesn't it? There are no words; you don't have to say anything. It's a very warm moment of understanding and reunion. Touching is a powerful form of communication.

We also send messages with our eyes. The way we look at someone can say a lot about our attitude. Eyes are a powerful means of communication.

Many of us have forgotten how to flirt with cur eyes, but do you remember all the things you could say with your eyes back when you were dating? Somebody clear across the room could get your message without a word being spoken.

It is very frustrating to talk to someone who won't look you in the eye. Did you ever notice that when you're having a family spat and you're angry with each other, you naturally avoid eye contact? You'll look at the floor or stare off into space. Why? Because there's tremendous intimacy in eye contact, and it's very difficult to communicate with somebody who will not look at you.

On the other hand, have you ever been around somebody who won't stop looking at you? Another interesting psychological experiment you may want to try sometime is to look directly at someone for a long time. Just decide that you're not going to break eye contact with a person. If you look a person in the eye long enough, the person will start checking out his or her clothing and looking all around to see what you're staring at. Try it.

Receiving no eye contact is disconcerting, but too much eye contact can be just as disconcerting. It can make a person very nervous. Eye contact is another form of nonverbal communication.

Body Language

How else do people communicate nonverbally? How about body language? In the early 1970s, Dr. Julius Fast wrote several books on the subject, describing the ways we communicate attitudes, emotions, feelings, ideas, and even specific messages by the way we sit, stand, or move various parts of our body.

Subsequently, Suzanne Szasz wrote two books on the body language of children, showing how adults (including parents and teachers) can understand the emotions and attitudes of kids by the way they move or position themselves.

There have been fascinating studies about how people protect the amount of space between them. This is a cultural phenomenon to some degree—people in Eastern nations have a very different sense of spatial and tactile relationships—but it is remarkably uniform within Western society. The distance between two people in conversation indicates all sorts of things—their level of friendship and intimacy, the degree of intensity or tension in the conversation, their respect for one another, etc.

How do you like it when somebody gets real close to

your face to talk to you? Bad breath suddenly becomes a major issue! But there's a lot more going on. Do you find that disconcerting? Unless it's a little child, most people feel very uncomfortable when a stranger moves into their private space.

Little children know something about this distancing almost instinctively. Have you ever noticed that when a child feels he hasn't got your undivided attention, he'll crawl up in your lap, rip the newspaper out of your hands, grab you by both ears, and get right up there in your face! He knows intuitively that when he gets in your space, he's got your attention!

Women, how do you feel when you want to have a heart-to-heart talk with your husband and he sits down across the room from you? You say, "Honey, I'd like to talk to you," and he sits on the sofa on the opposite wall. Much is communicated before anything is said. You need to be close to deal with a personal issue.

The spatial relationship has a lot to do with communication before anything verbal is ever said. Turning away, positioning the arms and legs, tilting the head, expressing with the eyes—all of these actions have meanings. Folding the arms across the chest is generally a sign of closing someone out; crossing the legs and folding the arms at the same time is a definite sign of freeze out.

Your Tone of Voice

Some very interesting studies have shown that only 7 percent of what is communicated between a husband and wife involves words. The first time I saw that research, I didn't believe it. The same study reported that 38 percent of communication involves tone of voice and inflection.

Did you ever stop to think how many different messages we can send using the exact same words in the exact same sequence? I'm sure you have played that game at one time or another, but consider the three most popular words in the English language, "I love you."

If I say those words to someone slowly and warmly, I communicate an idea of romantic love. But if I say them with a sarcastic tone, I can express the exact opposite meaning. I can also say the phrase in a casual way, as we often do to friends or fellow church members, and express a broad and general sense of loving someone. The three words have very different meanings, depending on how they're spoken. By changing the tone and inflection of my voice, I can change the message.

A husband comes home at night, and his wife meets him at the door. She says, "I didn't think you'd ever get home." If her tone of voice is forceful and accusatory, he hears one thing. But if she comes and says the same thing, "I didn't think you'd ever get home," with a tender, expectant tone of voice, suddenly romance is in the air!

We know those things instinctively; we use language in that way to communicate with friends and family. But it is still surprising how often we behave as if we do not know how we sound to each other. (Remember the first time you ever heard a recording of yourself, and you swore it wasn't you?) If we could hear how we sound to others—and modify our tone of voice accordingly—I doubt if we'd have nearly as much strife in our homes and places of business as we do today.

"Don't talk to me in that tone of voice." Have you ever said that to your children? Have you ever wanted to say that to your spouse? Your spouse may not even know that he or she is using a particular tone of voice because we don't always know how we sound to another person. Part of what we have to work on—and it does take work—

is to make sure that we're in sync in our message-sending abilities. It's not always easy, is it? We don't always know how we sound. But also, we don't always mean things the way our listeners hear them.

The Weight of the Nonverbal

It's fascinating to me that 45 percent of what we hear in marriage involves words, tone of voice, and inflection, but only 7 percent of that is actual choice of words. It's how we say the words and all the other things we communicate. Fully 55 percent—that is, most of what we hear in a conversation—is actually due to some form of nonverbal communication.

It's very important to understand that nonverbal communication generally overrides the verbal and carries more weight for the listener. It doesn't matter what we are saying with our lips if the nonverbal message is communicating something else.

Healthy communication means that we have learned to coordinate the verbal with the nonverbal. When we learn how to do that, truly dynamic communication can occur. When the message I say to you in words is reinforced by my tone of voice, inflection, and all the other nonverbal clues, it can be very powerful.

If you want to prove this for yourself, the next time you have a spat with your spouse or your best friend, try turning your back on each other and talking to each other that way. Make a mental note of your feelings and what's going on with your emotions. Then turn and face each other, take each other by the hand, and talk. See what happens. If you're having a bad argument with the person, you may not feel like doing all this. But if you do, you will immediately discover how the dynamics of touch and nonverbal communication either reinforce or alter the message.

If a man knows that his wife is a meticulous house-keeper and that she is very particular about how the house looks at all times, he can say, "Honey, I really love you. You're the greatest thing since 'Monday Night Football.'" But if he goes off to work leaving a trail of devastation everywhere he has been, how will she feel about those sweet words? The coffee cup is sitting on the dresser; his socks are draped over the lamp shade; his pajamas and other unmentionables are on the floor in a heap; shoes are scattered hither and yon. Which is she most likely to hear— what he said or what he did? And she will probably say to herself, "If you really love me, why can't you . . . ?" He needs to be more sensitive to what matters to her. His nonverbal message outweighed his verbal message.

The Sound of Silence

Words are dynamite, but they are not necessarily the key to what we hear from each other in marriage. There are many, many ways other than with words to communicate with each other. In fact, it is critical to realize that we are always communicating something, even when we are absolutely silent. We can't *not* communicate.

Couples often come in to me and say, "We're not communicating."

I have to ask them, "What do you mean?"

"Well," the wife will reply, "he won't talk to me."

So I ask her, "What do you hear when he won't talk to you?"

"I hear he doesn't think I'm bright enough to handle it. He doesn't think I'm smart enough to discuss it." The fact is, she is hearing all kinds of things, isn't she? Silence can be a deadly form of communication.

Remember the tragedy of the space shuttle disaster in Florida, when schoolteacher Christa McAuliffe and six NASA astronauts were killed? At lift-off, everybody was excited because history was being made. But then there was an explosion, and slowly we realized that we had witnessed a horrible tragedy.

When it became clear what had happened, the television cameras immediately began focusing on the various groups of people watching the scene. It was touching, but do you remember the reactions? Absolute silence. It was as if people were stunned beyond sound.

Sometimes we cannot think of words to express what we are feeling. But that doesn't mean that we feel nothing. There may be incredibly powerful emotions at work; emotions so strong that no words can capture them. There was almost no way to watch a disaster like that and put words to it.

Silence can be a powerful form of communication. But how do we usually interpret silence? Positively or negatively? Generally we think of it as negative. It is interesting that in our culture, when someone is deliberately quiet around us, we automatically assume the person is upset or angry. When we're left to interpret silence because we can't read the other person's mind, we almost always interpret it in some negative way, which can be a totally wrong and unfair conclusion.

Sometimes people just need silence. They may be off into their own world, their own thoughts. It may have nothing to do with their spouse or family. But if they don't somehow communicate that to the spouse, then he or she may get nervous and start imagining all kinds of reasons why the wife or husband isn't talking. The fear that arises can easily breed anger and antagonism.

If I go home after a long day and Jan is in a quiet, reflective mood, it's helpful to me if she says, "Honey, I've had a bad day at the shop. It has nothing to do with you, but I really just kind of need to be by myself for a while. I'm not feeling very social tonight, OK?"

I don't have a problem with that. I can say, "I understand, Dear. I know how you feel." Because she has cued me about her need for peace and quiet, I'm not left to guess about it and try to interpret her meaning. If she doesn't tell me what she feels, however, I may wander around the house wondering what I've done. Who knows what miseries I might dredge up? So sometimes we need to warn each other about our feelings.

Getting It All Out

I used to travel extensively. One time I got on the airplane and a woman sat down beside me. She was meticulously dressed, wearing a beautiful two-piece suit. She looked like she'd just stepped off the cover of *Vogue* magazine.

Every hair was perfectly in place. But the moment she sat down I knew she was a novice flyer. Stiff as a board and with eyes wide open, she squeezed those armrests like she was holding on for dear life. Her knuckles were absolutely white, and her face was the picture of anxiety.

I was feeling bad for her, so I tried to put her at ease with a little humor. But that didn't help much. She just stared straight ahead.

It wasn't long before we were airborne. After a few minutes, the flight attendants proceeded to serve lunch. Within minutes, my seatmate proceeded to give it right back. Unfortunately, she didn't know about the little bags in the seat back, so she took her best shot.

I will say this about her. She had impeccable aim. She didn't get a single drop on her beautiful suit. Instead, she threw up all over me. Well, I probably could have lived with that, except that after plastering me from head to foot, she said, "Gee, I feel better."

I looked at her with sheer wonder in my eyes. (I'm sure my nonverbal communication was working very well at that point.) I said: "Dear lady, you may feel better, but I'm sitting in it."

Once the drama of the moment had passed, I thought about that event and realized that is the way a lot of people behave. They vomit all over somebody verbally, get it "off their chest," so to speak. Then they have the nerve to say, "Well, I feel better now." But the other person is still sitting in it.

I know that was an awfully graphic illustration, and I apologize. But I think the analogy is so apt! I hope you will forgive me for using it, but I want to make a point: it is important, psychologically, that you express yourself, but you really need to do it in a sensible way.

I suspect that you know what I'm talking about. In the 1970s the big slogan of the younger generation was, "Let it all hang out." And, if you ever listened to them talk to each other during those years and even later, you would know what they meant.

Jan used to say, "These kids aren't going to grow up with any ulcers." I'd answer, "They're not going to grow up with any friends either," because people only like to be vomited on just so much. If they have any self-preservation skills, they start to put some distance between themselves and the upchucker.

We have learned that if we've got something going on

inside of us, it's important to get it out. No one is opposed to us getting our feelings out, providing we do it responsibly. But there is a limit to how much freedom we have in purging ourselves on someone else.

There are plenty of ways to explore what's going on inside of us without throwing up all over someone. I think Scripture expresses that idea when it says to "speak the truth in love," and "a soft answer turns away wrath." It is not an easy skill to master. From childhood on, we figure out that whenever we run headlong into a major problem, we should blame the other person first. Right?

Suppose I say to Jan: "Jan, you are an insensitive clod." Now, in a moment of anger, I may very well think that to be true. But what would have a better chance of getting Jan's sympathetic response—that statement, or something like: "Jan, I am really hurting"?

The latter, obviously. But why? In both instances I feel wounded or neglected. But with the first statement, I am attacking and doing deliberate damage to Jan's self-esteem; whereas, with the second one, I am admitting my vulnerability and asking for compassion. I have a much better chance of getting Jan's cooperation by sharing my feelings than by attacking hers.

Practicing the "I" Messages
When you have a dispute, you need to respond "I," not "You." But if you're not already accustomed to thinking this way, you'll have to practice. It may take you six months to break your old habits and learn a new way of behavior as your natural response.

In the meantime, while you're learning (and giving yourself some time), I would suggest that you memorize some time-buying statements; these are your best protection in bad situations.

Here are some gems that will help get you out of hot water. Statements such as, "I need time to sort this out." Or, "I'm too angry to deal with this right now." Or, "I'd like to think about this before I answer you."

These cop-outs can't be used in every conversation; your spouse will catch on very quickly. But you can say, "I don't know how to handle this." That's a time-buying statement. Or, "Would you let me think about this before responding?" These statements can be very helpful in dealing with teenagers. Believe me, you will need some of these time-buying statements when you have teenage kids.

Take curfew for example. Let's say curfew is at 10 P.M., and your daughter comes in at 2 A.M.. Ring any bells? At about eleven o'clock, you begin to get scared for the girl, imagining every kind of horror. But at two o'clock, when she suddenly appears, in a microsecond your fear turns into rage. In your mind you had her under a car in a ditch somewhere, and here she comes walking through the door, healthy and devilish. Instant rage!

So what do you normally do? Buy time? No. Instead you blurt out something totally irrational, like, "You're grounded for six years." Then you start that long, painful practice called backpedaling. By the next morning the sentence has been reduced to six months; by the following morning six weeks; by the next morning it's six days, and that may not stick. How much better it would be to buy a little time while you review your parental options.

You've got to rehearse these responses; they don't come naturally. But I'm deadly serious about this. You need this trick! If you don't memorize the statements and practice them to the point that they come naturally, you won't stand a chance. The only way to respond correctly is to rehearse the situations in your mind. You can practice them with your spouse. So here's your sixteen-year-old ballerina coming in at two in the morning, and now that your drooling hysteria has settled into a livid rage, what do you say?

Believe me, the conversation needs to be carefully rehearsed, but it should go something like this:

"What time did you understand curfew to be?"

"Ten."

"And what time is it now?"

"Two o'clock."

"That's very upsetting because we had all agreed on this. I am too angry to deal with this right now, so I want you to go on to your room and we'll talk about this later today."

Do you see how sensible that was? And part of the punch line is that they have to wait while you think about it. But at least you'll get to back off, get back in touch with your rational side, and let your spouse help you think it through before delivering your sentence.

It will also save you a lot of embarrassment. That's an example of a time-buying statement. So why should you learn this? Because if you don't, you will slip naturally into assaulting another person in the heat of anger, and that will only lead to escalating the confrontation. We need to be able to deal with our irritation and anger in a constructive way.

Confronting Your Anger

Can you remember a time when your spouse said something to you that just ripped your heart out? You're not sure why, but for some reason it wounded you very deeply. Chances are you had to pull yourself back a little to get in touch with what you were feeling at that moment, particularly if all your life you have been taught to attack and blame the other person first.

Your natural response would be to lash back: "You are a clod. You are a turkey. You are an insensitive clown." That's so much easier to do than to say, "Hey, whoa. I'm in pain. I'm hurting." But the second response is absolutely essential if you want healthy communications.

If you want the other person to spend his or her energy on listening rather than on defense, then forget the insult, lay off the invective, and look inward.

When the Scripture tells us to "speak the truth in love," you can believe that it is actually in your long-term best interest to learn to do it. And when the Scripture says, "A soft answer turns away wrath," it's in your long-term best interest to practice that approach. Of course, it works best when both people understand the process.

David and Vera Mace are very challenging and instructive writers and speakers on many of these subjects. Their books *Marriage: East and West* (Doubleday, 1960) and *The Sacred Fire: Christian Marriage through the Ages* (Abingdon, 1986) are fine resources. I especially recommend one of their tapes on this subject ("How to Have a Happy Marriage," Abingdon, 1977), which is a conversation about the love-anger cycle that every marriage experiences.

They explain that when two people are in love with each other and feeling warm and cozy toward each other, they are drawn toward each other. But when one of them does something that irritates the other one, they get angry, and the anger pushes them apart.

In time, if they have a normal, healthy marriage, they get over it and start feeling loving and warm, and they start drawing closer and closer together until one of them does something irritating again. That's why this is called the love-anger cycle. It is natural and, the Maces suggest, it is an inevitable cycle.

That kind of up and down relationship can make even the most stable couples feel as though their marriage is on a roller coaster. In one of their books, David and Vera Mace suggest ways of dealing with these ups and downs.

It is especially helpful to know that this very proper British couple has struggled with these problems in their own marriage—at least in the early days. The fact that they're now in their eighties and still happily married is pretty good evidence that their ideas work.

Perhaps the most essential part of their strategy is to acknowledge that there is a natural love-anger cycle and that an occasional battle does not mean they are hopelessly incompatible. What they did in their own marriage was to give each other permission to be angry. That's a very important thing to do because we all get angry with our spouses at times.

If you have never gotten angry with your spouse, either you're very sick or one of you is dead! Seriously, I often tell young couples not to get married until they've had a couple of good fights. Until they do battle, they're not dealing with reality.

There are times when couples don't like each other, but true love will survive the battles. If the couple's love can't survive the battle, it wasn't meant to be. It's better to find that out before the knot is tied.

Jan and I still love each other, though at times we may not like each other. Charlie Shedd tells about the first time he got a letter from his wife. It said, "Dear Charlie, I hate you. Love, Martha." That's the way life is.

Disappointment and anger are inevitable in any relationship, including our relationship to God. One of the most compelling books I have read in the past few years is called *Disappointment with God,* by Philip Yancey (Zondervan, 1989), which explores this situation in depth. If anyone tells me that he or she has never been angry with God, I question the seriousness of his or her relationship with him.

But what makes the principles discussed by David and Vera Mace refreshing is that they not only admit the anger, but they also deal with it immediately. They propose that whenever one spouse becomes angry with the other, he or she should tell the other about it.

Using their example, Vera would say something like, "David, I am very angry with you right now." David can deal with that. He doesn't panic or think Vera is going to divorce him. They both understand that anger is a normal part of the marriage relationship. And they have agreed to confront the anger whenever it appears, instead of going off and pouting about it. They made a commitment that they would verbalize their feelings to each other and attempt to clear the air.

Another commitment they made was to back off and process the cause of their anger. "Not only am I angry with you," Vera might say, "but I will work on discovering and finding out why I'm angry." And then, the final commitment is to come back together after they have thought about what made them angry, and talk it out.

Doesn't that seem like a healthy way to deal with anger? If every relationship is going to experience the love-anger cycle, shouldn't we have a built-in mechanism for dealing with it? You need to work on keeping the amount of time that anger pushes you apart to a minimum so that the hours of intimacy and closeness will be greater and much more significant.

I have heard couples say how very liberating it was for them to know that it's all right to be angry with their spouses from time to time. Many Christians are afraid that getting upset or angry with their mates is somehow sinful and shameful. They believe that anger is sin. But that is not true. Anger can certainly lead you to sin, and very quickly. But if dealt with promptly and lovingly, anger can be constructive and instructive in a marriage.

Have you ever heard the expression "Never go to bed angry"? Horseradish! If that were the case, you would never get any sleep. The Bible does not say that. It says, "Do not let the sun go down on your wrath" (Ephesians 4:26). That refers to anger that has become destructive. "Wrath" is anger that leads to hurting others, whether emotionally or physically, and the Scripture says we should put away wrath, malice, and other similar attitudes.

But if anger is sin, we have an interesting theological problem because Jesus got angry, and God gets angry. That would give us a sinning Savior and a sinning God. And that's impossible!

Anger, as an emotion, is not moral or immoral. In fact, we often call constructive anger *righteous indignation.* There are clearly matters that we ought to get angry about. Anger is a legitimate, though explosive, emotion. It is important to recognize our anger and have a system for dealing with it.

In giving permission to be angry, the Mace's method is healthy, productive, and practical, and I wholeheartedly recommend it. Remember, it calls for commitment. First, there's the commitment to verbalize disappointments right up front; second, the commitment to back off and get in touch with the reasons for our anger; third, the commitment to come back together and talk about it; and finally, the commitment to grow together in love and not to allow unhealthy emotions to become barriers.

In the next chapter we will deal with the subject of intimacy in marriage. But it is crucial to understand that until we learn to deal with our differences, we won't be able to experience true intimacy.

Love is a wonderful and mysterious emotion; it is an aspect of God himself. But love is not some mushy, wimpy emotion that has to tiptoe around the facts. It is a healthy and robust emotion committed to a total and vibrant relationship. That means there will be some disagreements and some differences from time to time.

Instead of being destructive, the differences can be constructive if we are truly committed to each other in love. Surely that is the way God meant for marriage to be.

| Six |

Intimacy—Too Close for Comfort?

We've been exploring verbal and nonverbal communication and the role each plays in a healthy marriage. At this point, I would like to look at some of the parallels between communication and intimacy in a marriage.

Again, I think it would be good to start with a portrait from the Scriptures. In Colossians 3, the apostle Paul dealt with subjects very much like those in Ephesians 4 and 5. Some very interesting passages precede Paul's very practical information about how wives and husbands are to relate to each other. It is also about how people are to relate to each other in all walks of life:

> Since you have been chosen by God who has given you this new kind of life, and because of his deep love and concern for you, you should practice tenderhearted mercy and kindness to others. Don't worry about making a good impression on them but be ready to suffer quietly and patiently. Be gentle

and ready to forgive; never hold grudges. Remember, the Lord forgave you, so you must forgive others.

Most of all, let love guide your life, for then the whole church will stay together in perfect harmony. Let the peace of heart which comes from Christ be always present in your hearts and lives, for this is your responsibility and privilege as members of his body. And always be thankful.

Remember what Christ taught and let his words enrich your lives and make you wise; teach them to each other and sing them out in psalms and hymns and spiritual songs, singing to the Lord with thankful hearts. And whatever you do or say, let it be as a representative of the Lord Jesus, and come with him into the presence of God the Father to give him your thanks. (Colossians 3:12-17, TLB)

Those are the verses that precede, "You wives, submit yourselves to your husbands, for that is what the Lord has planned for you. And you husbands must be loving and kind to your wives and not bitter against them nor harsh. You children must always obey your fathers and mothers, for that pleases the Lord" (Colossians 3:18-20, TLB). That is the context, and that should help set the tone for the kind of practical, interdependent relationship that is supposed to exist in marriage.

In chapter 2, we talked about some of the differences between males and females. Next we looked at healthy families. Then we discussed how to develop listening skills. And then we explored our Christian responsibility to learn how to package things: that is, to speak the truth in love, based on the biblical concept that "a soft answer turns away wrath."

If you have read any of John Powell's books, you know

that he is a marvelous writer. He is Roman Catholic priest, a Jesuit, who has written a number of books including, *Why Am I Afraid to Tell You Who I Am?* and *Why Am I Afraid to Love?* One of his books of which I am especially fond is *The Secret of Staying in Love.* I think some of his observations would be especially relevant to the focus of this work.

In *Why Am I Afraid to Tell You Who I Am?* Powell says that people communicate on five different levels. Whether it's husband to wife, parent to child, peer to peer, businessperson to businessperson, or whomever, we all interact on these levels.

Intimacy and Communication

In reading Powell's book some years ago, I came to the conclusion that the level of intimacy and closeness that people experience in a healthy marriage is directly related to the level at which they communicate with each other. The first level of communication Father Powell calls "Cliché Conversation." We use it all the time. It goes like this: "Hi. How ya doing? How's it going? Have a nice day."

Those are civil, somewhat Christian ways to say to people, "I acknowledge that you breathe and take up space and occupy a certain molecular structure." Instead of ignoring each other or being crass and unfeeling, we resort to clichés and very simple, common expressions to acknowledge one another.

If you don't believe it, the next time somebody says, "Hi, how's it going?" try to tell them very specifically and in appropriate detail how it is going. I suspect you will discover very quickly that the greeting was not meant to be an invitation to closeness. Rather, it was a way to acknowledge and greet you.

That's all right, of course. We cannot move into inti-

macy or closeness with everybody we meet. We simply
are not built that way. So to maintain civility and deco-
rum, we tend to hold most people at arm's distance by
saying, "Hey, I acknowledge that you are there, and I see
you, but that's all I want."

Level two, according to Powell, is what he calls "Report-
ing the Facts." This is a sharing of information. This is the
United States of America, planet Earth, somewhere in
middle America in the late twentieth century. Facts. Nothing threatening about these, nothing revolutionary. And
if you want to make sense out of the newspaper tonight,
you might need to know the facts.

There's no emotional risk at that level of conversation.
But we need information from people, so we sometimes
communicate just on a "need for information" basis. We
have the need for the facts.

Level three, is the first level where there may be an
emotional threat. It's the "Opinion or Judgment" level.
Let's see if I can demonstrate that. I live in Dallas, Texas,
the home of the Dallas Cowboys football team. That's
information. If I say that I think they stunk last season,
that's an opinion.

The moment I move from information to opinion, I
risk getting into an argument. Some other Cowboys fan
(or one of the players or coaches) may have thought they
were "just plumb near wonderful!" Though I may question that person's sanity on such a conclusion, that is
their opinion, and they're certainly entitled to it. Nevertheless, the moment I share my opinion with you, we can
come into conflict with each other.

Did you ever know anyone who didn't have an opinion about anything? Or if he did, he kept it to himself?
What he learned early in his childhood was that *you don't
share an opinion because it's too emotionally risky.*

Somewhere, sometime, he shared an opinion, and somebody else discounted it. In other words, somebody clobbered him for it, or somebody shot him down. Sometimes that vulnerability will continue right into marriage. A wife expresses her opinion on an issue, and right away her husband retorts, "That's the stupidest thing I've ever heard. Where in the world did you come up with that idiotic idea?" So she makes a mental note and says, "Well, no more sharing of opinions with him. Too risky."

So level three of John Powell's thesis is conversation about an opinion or a judgment.

Feelings and Emotions

Level four gets even scarier, since it involves sharing personal feelings and emotions. It is the "Feelings" level. At this level, you're really taking a chance, because when you share your feelings, you hand the other person a weapon. That person can either use your personal revelation as a weapon against you, or they can use it as a tool to help you. At any rate, those who know your personal emotions have specific insight into who you are and what you're all about. We touched on this in the last chapter.

Finally, level five is the "Gut" level. This is complete emotional and personal self-disclosure. Now we're talking heavy duty risk. At this level there is nothing going on inside of me—absolutely nothing—that I'm afraid to share with you.

I suspect that level five communication takes place with very few people. In fact, very few times is that level of intimacy ever achieved in marriage. It's too scary. It's too risky. The problem is that a happy and healthy marriage has got to get to at least level four (that is, the expression of feelings and emotions) and stay there most of the time.

An incredibly good marriage will touch level five. This is where there is so much trust that no matter what fantasy or fear you reveal, no matter what hopes and dreams you may harbor, and no matter who you are on the inside, you feel absolutely free to be open with your spouse. Then you will be willing to risk everything with him or her because you have learned that he or she can deal with the information. If you are fortunate enough to have reached this level with your spouse, you have an incredible and rare relationship.

Knowing that we have such intimacy with another person will create an incredibly close bond. Some people develop that with another friend. I understand that some women reach this level with friends now and then. But one thing seems clear: if you ever have a friendship where there is complete, emotional self-disclosure, that relationship will be thicker than blood.

Nevertheless, it's scary business, and you never know if the other person can deal with it until you take a chance. Perhaps the greatest risk is that if they cannot be trusted at that level of intimacy, you may discover the fact too late, after you've bared your soul.

Whenever we tell people about our feelings and emotions, we really become vulnerable, don't we? But dealing with self-disclosure is a trust—I might even say a sacred trust. If we do not learn to handle self-disclosure—especially with our spouses—they will invariably quit self-disclosing because they have discovered that it's too risky. It isn't safe!

Confession and Forgiveness
I believe that all of us have a need to self-disclose. Why else would God ask us to be honest with him? Why does the Lord have us confess our sins to him? God already

has access to that information, so there must be another reason.

If we are Christians, self-disclosure is an emotional release of troubling facts and emotions. The Bible says, "If we confess our sins, He [God] is faithful and just to forgive us our sins and to cleanse us from all unrighteousness" (1 John 1:9). This assures us that there is *safety* when we confess to God. We have a promise that our deepest, most heartfelt emotions will be heard by Almighty God with mercy.

When believers confess to God—and I hope you understand this, for it is such a great comfort—there is an atmosphere of safety and mercy because of the finished work of Christ. Christ has already paid our debt. And when we confess to God and know that he has heard our confession with grace and mercy, we experience genuine cleansing. We receive God's own promise of forgiveness, and the sense of cleansing and forgiveness makes us feel close to him. So confession—self-disclosure—is linked to feeling close to God. It isn't that God needs the information. He already knows it. We need to confess in order to experience closeness with him.

When we open up to our spouses, we need the same sense of safety and mercy, or we won't do it. Of course, there are things that are not wise to share with your spouse. Some things may be so frightening, scary, and threatening to your spouse that they simply cannot be shared. That's always a judgment call, and it's a tough one. But I would suggest that what draws people together in the first place is a certain feeling of comfort, a sense that it is safe to share personal feelings with this individual.

Caring and Sharing

In Western culture, we have a kind of supermarket approach to marriage. By that I mean we go down the aisles and squeeze the tomatoes, choose what we want, and pay at the other end. In the Oriental cultures, on the other hand, where marriage is still often arranged by the parents and grandparents, you don't marry the person you choose. Partners are not picked on the basis of intimacy or for their capacity for sharing personal emotions.

But in our culture, where we date and go through romance and courtship, one of the things that tends to draw people together is self-disclosure. Often couples come to see me at the office and say, "Golly, before we got married, we could talk about anything. We talked for hours. Now we can't talk about anything."

I always wonder what happened, but I have a good hunch. Before people are married, self-disclosure is not so frightening. After marriage, however, emotions, secret dreams, and deeply held fears take on much greater force. What our spouses know about us is intimately related to our future security and our beliefs about everything we possess.

For example, if you are married, think back to when you were just dating. Or you may be dating now and exploring the pros and cons of married life, but you also understand these emotions.

Did you ever go to a party single, and then wished you hadn't gone? You're sitting there feeling like a wart. You're ready to ease your way toward the door, and you're waiting for the right moment to slip out.

But somebody comes up, and you say hello. What level are you on? Level one.

"Hello."

"Hello."

So he sits down beside you, and a very small conversation begins.

"Hello, my name's Tom Timid."

"Hi, my name's Betty Bashful," or whatever. "I'm a public school teacher."

That's all safe, isn't it? You've just shared some information. You've taken no risk. It may end there. And you both slip out into the dark.

But suppose you say, "Before you came up and sat down beside me, I was thinking about slipping out into the dark. I'm kind of an introvert." What that other person does with that information makes or breaks the evening. Suppose the person stands up on the coffee table and says, "May I have everyone's attention. I've just met an introvert. Everybody gather around and make this introvert feel welcome." Right there, on the spot, you would be prepared to kill that person, wouldn't you?

But suppose it goes a different way. You explain that you're kind of introverted and very uncomfortable at parties like this. He says, "Me, too."

All of a sudden you have something in common—which, incidentally, is the root of the word *commun*-ication. And, depending on how he receives information, you may even find yourself sharing things with that person you haven't told some of your best friends. That might lead in turn to, "Hey, I'd kind of like to go out with you."

So you have a date and you share more. Then another date and you share more. You begin to realize that you can talk about anything. The person doesn't get out his prayer list and make notes. He doesn't fall off the chair in shock. He doesn't pass judgment. He just listens.

All of a sudden you find yourself tremendously attracted to him. You think, *This is the way I'd like to spend the rest of my life. Here is somebody really neat who accepts me, warts and all—someone who can be trusted with my self-disclosure.*

You get interested in somebody like that. At that point, then, the sexual dynamic enters in. Before you know it, you're planning to get married. What has drawn you together? Your need to self-disclose and your being accepted by somebody else, with mercy. And you decide this is the person you want to spend your life with.

I believe God has built into each of us the need to be transparent with at least one other human being and to know that, however deep and personal we may become, we are safe with that person.

Changing Dynamics

Ironically, as we noted earlier, the personal dynamic changes after marriage. Suddenly there's a risk. Now there's a bigger investment. Two people have put a home together; they've merged their bank accounts; they may have a child. There's a whole lot involved.

Suppose that, after a time, something happens to the husband—a concern or problem. It may be something scary and spooky; something he's not really proud of. He wonders if his wife can handle this information. He comes to the conclusion that she can't, and he starts to hide from her.

You know something? A lot of marriages hit that roadblock and never recover. The couple at that point retreats to level one or two. They're civil. They live under the same roof. It's like the functional marriage I mentioned in chapter 1—their lives touch, but there's nothing going on.

The couples who go back to levels one and two decide to settle for safe, defined roles. I'll do this, you do that, we'll share the expenses, live under the same roof, but that's as far as it goes.

So when I say that it's very important to learn how to handle information, I mean that there is a direct correlation between our ability to handle self-disclosure and the degree of intimacy in the relationship.

The more emotional self-disclosure that takes place in a marriage, the closer the husband and wife will feel to each other. That is a cardinal rule. But emotional self-disclosure is risky. Things that may be fairly simple for a stranger to understand may be much more threatening to our spouse simply because our spouse has an enormous emotional investment in us. Our futures and our safety are so intimately linked. We need to recognize that when we share with one another.

As I said earlier, one of the reasons affairs get started is that people sometimes find that they can talk about certain areas more easily with somebody who isn't married to them than they can with their own spouse. Clearly, a stranger or a friend not related to them is not nearly as threatened by personal details as their spouse would be.

In chapter 2, we saw that one of the basic differences between men and women is that women tend, first of all, to be in touch with their feelings, and then with their thoughts. Men tend to be into their thoughts first, and only later with their feelings. By and large, men do not tend to self-disclose as quickly as women who have been conditioned from infancy to feel that it's OK to be in touch with their feelings and emotions and to verbalize them.

For many men, feelings can be deep and threatening. Often they don't know how to verbalize those feelings as well as women. Women have had so much more training in it. In fact, that's why women will consider going to counselors more readily than men: counseling is a part of self-revelation. Self-disclosure is more natural for them.

That kind of disclosure is scary stuff for many men. But one of the things we are taught, in our training as counselors, is how to deal with people's self-disclosure in order to create a safe environment for the client so that he or she will be more willing to open up. The dynamics of this process are fascinating but demanding.

If you are going to have closeness in your marriage, and if you want to have that interrelatedness—those overlapping circles where there is something of value going on between the two of you—you will have to learn how to talk to each other about your feelings. You also have to learn how to listen to each other, and how to accept the other's feelings.

Learning to Talk

It is important to learn how to communicate freely with our spouse. No one wants to feel like the whole world has to be caving in before anybody will listen. So we should learn to talk even when there's no crisis.

Remember that *intimacy is an ebb and flow experience.* You are not always going to feel pink passion for your spouse. Have you found that out yet? The marriage is not always going to be red hot. In fact, you couldn't take it if it were.

The truth is, there will be times when you won't even like your spouse. It doesn't mean you will stop loving him or her, but you simply won't like the person at that moment. That's all right. It is a very natural response.

The same is true in a relationship with God. Do you always feel close to God? I doubt it. People in the Bible didn't always feel close to him. Many of them grew discontented, even angry with God. Many of them were holy men and women, but their feelings and their intimate relationships with him would ebb and flow with the events and emotions of their lives. Again, that's OK. God understands.

If you just read Psalms, you will see how King David's feelings fluctuate from one paragraph to the next. In Psalm 21 he wrote, "The king shall have joy in Your strength, O Lord; and in Your salvation how greatly shall he rejoice! You have given him his heart's desire" (Psalm 21:1-2). Talk about a high! But then, in the very next psalm he wrote, "My God, My God, why have You forsaken Me? Why are You so far from helping Me, and from the words of My groaning?" (Psalm 22:1). It means he's in the pits. One moment he feels like he's walking hand in hand with God, and the next moment he thinks God has gone on a vacation and left the phone off the hook.

It is also important to notice that this is the same passage recited by Christ on the cross in the hour of his death. No one is impervious to pain and aloneness.

All our relationships will ebb and flow. It is our commitment to each other that keeps us together in the ebb. The warm fuzzies will take care of the flow. But it takes commitment to protect a marriage through all the ebbs and flows of life.

How do you deal with those times when you don't feel very warm toward your spouse? And the times when your spouse doesn't feel very warm or close to you?

The corollary to closeness is a healthy sense of identity. That means that husbands and wives need to *learn to leave space for each other.* Again, going back to the circles we created in chapter 1, we know that in a healthy marriage both partners have their own sense of identity and autonomy. Part of their autonomy is in knowing who they are apart from their spouse, as well as who they are together.

The Scripture calls this "oneness." You are one in marriage, but it is okay to be apart for hours at a time. Your spouse does not have to have you around twenty-four hours a day. Each partner needs his or her own sense of identity apart from the marriage.

If you are a homemaker, you may find yourself trying to put all your emotional eggs in your husband's basket. Then you can't understand why you get depressed so easily when he wants to go somewhere alone or when he ignores you around the house. If you want to avoid that trap, you've got to leave space for each other. You need your private time; so does your husband.

There are times when I say to Jan, "Darling, I need some time alone. I can't deal with any new demands on me right now." We take family vacations together; but we also take independent vacations. Each year, Jan takes a week of vacation by herself, to refresh and recharge her batteries. I take a short vacation by myself as well.

This year Jan went to Kansas to spend some time with one of her female friends. A couple of years ago she went to Natchez, Mississippi, and visited all those remodeled plantation homes. That's her idea of a good time!

For me, a vacation like that would be about as pleasant as a root canal without Novocain. I'd like an historic tour about as much as Jan would like going to Wyoming with me, camping out in ten-degree weather and sleeping in a tent.

But that's all right. I need time alone, with no demands. Eleven months of the year I am a minister, counselor, father, and husband. Eleven months of the year Jan is a mother, wife, and businesswoman. We both need time apart, just as we need time together.

Time Management

Time needs to be negotiated continually, but if you can't bear the idea of time apart from your mate, you may be enmeshed in your marriage. We have already observed that a compulsive attachment to your mate is not healthy.

It is important for us to *have some form of activity and involvement outside the marriage.* I certainly do not mean to suggest that anyone should have an affair! I mean that you need some source of activity and fulfillment in your life that is not directly related to the marriage.

One of the real dangers for homemakers is allowing their time with the children and their activities to take the place of their own personal time. There are two problems with that: first, the woman makes no time for herself to recharge, to be herself, to talk to other adults; second, she gets so much affection from her kids that she robs her spouse of attention and affection. Homemakers must be careful of that.

The divine order for all of us is that God must be first in our lives, our spouses second, and our children third. Your spouse cannot take the place of God in your life, but the children must not come before your husband or wife. Remember that your marriage is your primary relationship in the home. Before the kids came, you were. And after the kids leave, hopefully you shall be.

If that is a potential problem in your life, Mom or Dad, remember that you are not doing your kids any favors by giving them greater importance than your spouse. For that matter, you are not doing your spouse or yourself any favors. You need a source of activity and involvement outside the marriage, but that source cannot be allowed to rob your mate or your family.

All of us need a good friend or some activity apart from

marriage that is satisfying and rewarding to us. Without some outside stimulation, we tend to allow all our emotional demands to fall on our spouse and children, and no one can carry that. That is a very unfair demand to put on any member of the family.

Another principle, very much in keeping with all we have been talking about in this book, is that *you need to educate yourself about the opposite sex.*

Now wait a minute! That is not as foolish as it sounds. It is very important. When I have asked women if they *understand* men, they admit they do not. Men readily admit they don't *understand* women. So why do we act as if we know all there is to know?

Not only must I, as a man, try to learn about women, but there is one particular woman that I had better educate myself about, and that's my wife. She is not like every other woman. Yes, there are a lot of things women have in common, but there are many ways that each individual woman is unique, different from all other women.

Believe it or not, women, you do not know as much about men as you think you do. It's true, as a rule, that women tend to know more about men than men know about women, but that's not everything. I know you have already discovered great dark areas in your mate or boyfriend that mystify you from time to time. Don't be surprised; it will always be that way.

Nevertheless, we need to try to educate ourselves about the opposite sex. The only way that can happen is for the opposite sex to tell us about themselves. We don't read minds, so we need constructive, creative, and open dialogue, seasoned with love, between men and women on a regular basis.

Barriers to Intimacy

What are some of the barriers to intimacy? Not surprisingly, there are several. You would think that being close to someone and sharing easily in an environment of intimacy would be simple and natural, wouldn't you? How I wish that were true! But there are many barriers. Let me name a few.

The first barrier to intimacy is *emotional immaturity*. All of us have areas where we're not emotionally mature. The second is *fear of being hurt*. If we were injured emotionally either in childhood or at some time earlier in our lives, we may be afraid to take risks now. Our difficulty in sharing our feelings can follow us into marriage.

In some cases, people get married and have a terrible experience. They get burned and then have real difficulty trusting anyone ever again. People like that have divided emotions. They want to trust their spouses, but they can't help being afraid of being hurt.

Sometimes the hurt runs incredibly deep. Many men, in particular, find emotional hurts like that to be a barrier to intimacy in their second marriage. Sometimes it takes prolonged and compassionate counseling to overcome the damage.

Others may have been hurt in a dating relationship before their first marriage. They may have been seriously hurt—dropped down the elevator shaft of love, so to speak—emotionally clobbered by someone they wanted to love. Some of them may carry deep scars from these broken romances.

That kind of suffering can easily follow us into a marriage relationship and leave us with a nagging fear of the opposite sex. I see the same thing in women who may have had real difficulties relating positively to their fathers. In many cases, women in this type of situation grow up afraid of men, afraid of sharing their emotions with a man.

We have to deal with such matters to overcome them. If there are pathological issues such as incest or abuse involved, then there will certainly be barriers to the amount of intimacy we can feel in all our relationships. Until there has been a period of constructive and recon-structive therapy, life will be difficult.

A man may have grown up in a home with a very dom-ineering mother. Consequently he may feel subcon-sciously that all women are out to castrate him, to put him down, and keep him in his place. So he's afraid to be vulnerable to a woman.

These situations sometimes produce what we call "ghost marriages." In these marriages, bad experiences from the past continue to haunt the person the rest of his or her life. A man haunted by his childhood, where the home was ruled by a domineering mother, may fre-quently feel that the things his wife is saying remind him of the things his mother used to say. Then, instead of dealing with his wife, he deals emotionally with his mother again, and he reacts inappropriately and usually in anger. Such situations can create enormous barriers to intimacy in the home.

Misplaced anger and hostility of this kind can be devas-tating to a marriage. Such anger can be found in both men and women. When a husband is picking on his wife, he may actually be dealing with something that he ought to work out with his mother.

A wife may be attacking her husband because of some phantom from the past, some resentment that she still holds for her father. You might be surprised just how com-mon this problem really is.

This type of misplaced anger is one of the major issues

we see in counseling. Both partners may have unsettled issues with their parents, but they fight with each other over ghosts from the past. The spouse isn't even involved, but the hostility swallows them and begins to create incredible barriers to intimacy and closeness.

Pseudo Intimacy

Other barriers to intimacy need to be addressed in this chapter before moving on to the issue of conflict resolution. The first is what I call *pseudo intimacy.* This is closeness without mutuality. It is, in fact, false intimacy.

There are some people who get close in order to manipulate. Sometimes sales people do this. They get close to people to manipulate them for their own ends—to make a sale. But it also happens in other relationships.

Over-socializing can be a barrier to intimacy. I know some couples who always have to have another couple around. They don't ever just go out one-on-one and enjoy each other. This is a distancing technique. As a result, they fail to learn how to relate as husband and wife. They try to substitute social life for intimacy.

Pseudo intimacy is intimacy with a hook in it, and the hook has a barb. That will not only create a barrier to intimacy but will wound and injure the person who gets snagged. Sexual intimacy without relatedness will destroy intimacy. I think this is very much the same issue.

God designed sexual intercourse to be the sacrament of emotional intimacy. You cannot get to emotional intimacy through sex. Rather, you get to sex through emotional intimacy. If you try to do it the other way around, you will fail every time.

That is the lesson the world is learning, ever so slowly, today. The world wants to believe that physical closeness will evolve into true love and emotional intimacy. Sorry, it doesn't work that way. God did not design it to work that way. And if you insist on pursuing that dream, you'll burn out your bearings chasing a myth.

Just consider what's happening in the hot spots and singles bars of our society. Watch the poor deluded people playing musical beds. There is enormous emptiness and heartbreak in that life-style, and it never leads to emotional closeness. It leads to feelings of being used and exploited; it leads to anger and hostility; it does not lead to love. It cannot, and it never will.

Physical intimacy without commitment, without relatedness, will create a barrier to closeness. The model God has given us involves sharing, spending time with each other, and being a part of each other's lives.

The Sexual Counterrevolution

In a *Time* magazine cover feature entitled "The Revolution is Over" (April, 1984), a New York City writer who reportedly slept with about two dozen women in the first months after his divorce is quoted as saying, "It's terrible to wake up and wonder why this person's head is on the other pillow. It was painful for them and me too."

The painful irony of the sex scene is that lonely people have convinced themselves that sex is the object when, in fact, they are really dying for a meaningful relationship. A Chicago bar owner also saw the irony and the duplicity of the sexual revolution, saying, "All the happy-go-lucky singles in my place tell me that they do not want a relationship; then six months later, they are engaged."

A businessman in the Boston area, going through a divorce, said he was swearing off the one-night stands. "I don't want it, don't need it, and don't believe in it. I hope to find one person to share my life with. Who doesn't?"

According to the magazine's report, even people in the "sex business" are observing a shift in attitudes and a return to more traditional values. San Francisco sex therapist Lonnie Barbach said, "We've been going through a Me generation: now I see people wanting to get back into the We generation."

A *Cosmopolitan* magazine survey found that "so many readers wrote negatively about the sexual revolution, expressing longings for vanished intimacy and the now elusive joys of romance and commitment that we began to sense that there might be a sexual counter-revolution under way in America."

Editor Helen Gurley Brown, never one to miss a sexual trend, said, "Sex with commitment is absolutely delicious. Sex with your date for the evening is not so marvelous—too casual, too meaningless."

In the same article, Manhattan sex therapist Shirley Zussman observed that her patients these days complain about the emptiness of sex without commitment. "Being part of a meat market is appalling in terms of self-esteem," she said. The writers suggested that "fears of both loneliness and intimacy are a backlash against the 'cool sex,' promoted during the sexual revolution."

Signs of the breakdown in the trendy sex revolution are showing up everywhere. Psychiatrist Domeena Renshaw, director of the Sexual Dysfunction Clinic at Chicago's Loyola University, has a waiting list of 200 couples seeking help. She stated that many of her patients have tried group sex and the swinging scene, but for them it has been "destructive and corrosive." Furthermore, she adds, "Often the partner who suggested it first is the one who suffers most."

The article ended with the following summary: "Though many values are still being sorted out, most

Americans seem stubbornly committed to family, marriage, and the traditional idea that sex is tied to affection or justified by it. 'Cool sex,' cut off from the emotions and the rest of life, seems empty, unacceptable or immoral."

Dr. David Scharff, a psychoanalyst and author of *The Sexual Relationship,* states, "The whole culture is on a swing back to more traditional expectations, there is a return to the understanding that the main function of sex is the bodily expression of intimacy" (quoted in *Time,* April 9, 1984).

The Bond of Oneness

This brings us back to marriage and physical intimacy within marriage. Once again, the differences between men and women need to be observed, and the idea of biblical *oneness* must be the standard of authentic sexual behavior in marriage.

Men and women naturally approach sex from very different perspectives. Men tend to be physically oriented, while women tend to be relationally oriented. This difference is not limited to their sexual relationship, but it certainly shows up there.

For example, a husband and wife may have had a fight and both are tired of fighting. He figures that having sex would be a great way to make up. But she wants to make up before they come together sexually. These are two very different attitudes and emotions.

Years ago, a national periodical summarized it this way: Men tend to give love in order to get sex; Women tend to give sex in order to get love.

Author Ingrid Trobisch stated it beautifully. She said, "A man is aroused by what he sees: a woman by what she hears. The greatest erogenous zone of a woman's body is her heart. It is the words she hears from her husband that reach her heart and 'open up' her body. For her, the sexual act is not an event with a definite beginning and an end. Rather, all that she does is enclosed in this atmosphere of love. Her thinking and feeling are centered on her husband even if she is working, preparing a meal, cleaning the house, doing the laundry or shopping. She cannot separate her body from her soul. That which she feels inside is the same as that which she expresses outwardly" (from "Male/Female Attitudes Toward Sex" in *Husbands and Wives* (Victor Books, 1988).

She states further: "In many ways, it is easier for a man to be satisfied sexually. He's thirsty, he takes a drink of water and then his thirst is quenched. A woman is thirsty, too, but in the moment she is ready to take a drink, the glass may fall and break into a thousand pieces through a cross word or a disappointment. If this happens, she is left with her thirst."

For a woman, emotional intimacy and physical intimacy are inseparable. This is not necessarily true for a man. You can have some very interesting conversations behind closed doors. An irate wife is heard to say, "How can you think of sex when we're not even speaking?" Her husband replies, "Well, couldn't we just do it without talking?" There is hardly an area of relationship between men and women that requires more understanding and forgiving than this one.

Sexual Issues

As a counselor, I find that most sexual issues (other than dysfunctional situations) fall into one of four categories. The first category concerns the issue of *frequency*. Men generally desire sexual contact more often than women, although I have counseled many couples where the opposite was true.

Women tend to respond as emotionally to a sense of closeness—being cherished, being held, being nurtured—as much as the sexual act itself. Women are often quite satisfied with touching, hugging, holding, and they may often desire these without any need of consummation in sexual intercourse. On the other hand, men tend to feel cheated if the act of intercourse is not included.

The second set of issues concerns what I would call *intensity,* or lack thereof. The feeling that your partner is not really present or involved can cause a lot of hard feelings. Some men complain that it seems like the woman is saying, "Here's my body. Give it back when you're finished with it."

A minister friend of mine often tells couples that sex in marriage is a lot like eating. Sometimes you may grab a snack on the run; sometimes you sit down to a regular dinner; but sometimes you want to enjoy a gourmet feast. To expect every sexual encounter to be a gourmet feast is illogical; but if every sexual encounter feels more like a "snack on the run," you're going to have trouble.

The third set of issues that couples bring to me involves *variety of sexual expression.* Again, generally speaking, men seem to want more variety of sexual expression than women, but I must quickly admit that this is not universal, and it is not uncommon for the woman to be the one who is looking for relief from the same routine.

A good rule of thumb regarding what is acceptable in sexual activity would seem to be that if it is not psychologically or physiologically damaging, and if both partners are open to it, go for it! In a healthy marriage, sexual variety may well be the spice of life. There is no reason for your sexual life to be deadly boring.

The fourth and final set of issues I commonly see involving sex in marriage concerns *communication*. Some couples can talk about anything in their relationship but sex. But not to be able to express what you like or don't like, enjoy or don't enjoy, wish to try or do not wish to try, can be frustrating at best and devastating at worst.

When the writers of the Old Testament alluded to the act of sexual intercourse, they commonly used the expression "to know" each other. I think that is an excellent word. Because so much of our femininity or masculinity can be tied up in our sexuality, it is imperative to "know" each other sexually, to take an interest in what pleases our mates, and to give each other the freedom to express our sexual natures in the union of marriage, as God clearly intended it.

When you are bonded with your spouse in that way, and when you are married in a divine union of love and commitment, I believe you will share the greatest treasure a man and woman can have together on this earth.

SEVEN

EVERYONE WINS IN A GOOD, CLEAN FIGHT!

That we all have conflicts in our relationships is probably one of the safest assumptions we can make. If you are alive (and you're not a monk or a hermit!), you are going to have conflict. You cannot have a personal relationship without it.

Conflict is not always bad. Sometimes the only way to get to the root of a serious problem is by reaching a certain level of anger. But there is a fine line between constructive and destructive anger, and once we cross that line our emotions can be very dangerous. Ann Landers once said, "Anger is like an acid that destroys its container"—that tends to be true.

To get some perspective on this issue, notice what the Bible says about how people are supposed to relate to each other in interpersonal relationships:

> Since you became alive again, so to speak, when Christ arose from the dead, now set your sights on the rich treasures and joys of heaven where he sits

131

beside God in the place of honor and power. Let
heaven fill your thoughts; don't spend your time
worrying about things down here. (Colossians 3:1-2,
TLB)

That seems like pretty good advice, doesn't it? If we
could just pull it off. Paul, the writer, continued:

You should have as little desire for this world as a
dead person does. Your real life is in heaven with
Christ and God. And when Christ who is our real life
comes back again, you will shine with him and share
in all of his glories. Away then with sinful, earthly
things; deaden the evil desires lurking within you;
have nothing to do with sexual sin, impurity, lust
and shameful desires; don't worship the good things
of life, for that is idolatry. God's terrible anger is
upon those who do such things. (Colossians 3:3-6,
TLB).

Isn't it interesting that God gets angry all through the
Scriptures? Obviously there is a time for righteous anger
just as there is a time for tolerance and patience. "You
used to do them when your life was still part of this
world; but now is the time to cast off and throw away all
these rotten garments of anger, hatred, cursing, and dirty
language" (Colossians 3:7-8, TLB).

So the Scripture is saying: "All right, believers, I expect
you to behave in a different way than nonbelievers. Is
that clear?"

Don't tell lies to each other; it was your old life with
all its wickedness that did that sort of thing; now it is
dead and gone. You are living a brand new kind of

life that is continually learning more and more of what is right, and trying constantly to be more and more like Christ who created this new life within you. In this new life one's nationality or race or education or social position is unimportant; such things mean nothing. Whether a person has Christ is what matters, and he is equally available to all.

Since you have been chosen by God who has given you this new kind of life, and because of his deep love and concern for you, you should practice tenderhearted mercy and kindness to others. Don't worry about making a good impression on them but be ready to suffer quietly and patiently. Be gentle and ready to forgive; never hold grudges. Remember, the Lord forgave you so you must forgive others.

Most of all, let love guide your life, for then the whole church will stay together in perfect harmony. Let the peace of heart which comes from Christ be always present in your hearts and lives, for this is your responsibility and privilege as members of his body. And always be thankful. (Colossians 3:9-15, TLB)

That's a lot easier to read than to practice, isn't it? Long-suffering is not a natural part of our human nature: it is a learned behavior. In the natural state, men and women tend to be highly defensive, guarding their own rights and autonomy.

It's not that people are like wolverines, constantly looking for ways to chew each other apart. But we have an instinct for self-preservation that applies not only to physical survival but to emotional survival as well. Whenever there is a disagreement, we are naturally inclined to hold fast to our own beliefs and challenge those of the other person. That is a basic psychological fact.

The Nature of Conflict

If I were to pick any two people, completely at random, and shut them up in a room together for a period of time, before very long some sort of conflict would arise. Conflict is inevitable for all living things. This may seem like a terribly broad statement, but it is true nonetheless. Conflict has always been a natural part of life since the beginning of time.

The Bible is full of conflict. In the beginning, people had conflict with God, and God had conflict with people. I don't have to tell you that people had conflict with each other. The record speaks only too clearly on that score. Cain and Abel's situation is not even the first or most serious example of conflict; but their story is evidence that bad blood goes back a very long way.

If there were no conflicts in a relationship, I would have to wonder if there is a relationship at all. As we discussed in chapter 5, that applies to our relationship with God as well. That's because conflict involves personal values and needs, and everybody brings different needs and values to the relationship.

Why is this true? First of all, our backgrounds are different. Regardless of who you are or where you come from, no two people were raised exactly the same, even if they are identical twins. Perceptions, reactions, and native emotions will always be unique and personal, so each person will have a slightly different belief system, a different set of values, different moods, and, more to the point, a different set of needs. This will be equally true in marriage, dating, work situations, peer relationships, or virtually any environment where people come together.

As a counselor, I would suggest that conflict emerges because most of us do not know how to deal openly and quickly with basic differences. In protecting our own values and emotions, we can be very intolerant of those whose opinions may differ from ours.

Dealing with Anger

How, then, do we normally deal with the emotions that arise in these situations? How do we deal with anger? Some people cope by denying that anger exists. Others suppress it. They say, "I'm not angry; I'm not upset." All the while they're boiling inside. Sound familiar?

Another more subtle way of dealing with anger and frustration is to get mad at somebody else. People will unleash their anger on somebody they know (such as a child or a spouse) rather than confront the person with whom they are angry.

Other ways? Ignore them. Just get quiet, really quiet. That's a form of withdrawal from another person. A lot of people handle conflict that way. They withdraw because they think it's the safest and quietest way to handle a problem.

Some people respond with humor. They laugh about the situation or frame it in a humorous way to make it seem a little less threatening. Others just try to be nice; they're all sugarcoated sweetness and light. Dripping with it. I think that may be the worst of all!

For many people, a more typical way of showing their emotions is by a sullen, emotional response. Sarcasm and disgust can be the most hurtful way of expressing irritation and anger. It may give the person a sense of getting even, but it doesn't solve the problem.

In any event, all of these reactions are evidence that we don't really know how to handle anger appropriately, yet the Scriptures instruct us to treat people with tenderheart-edness, with loving-kindness. We are told to forgive one another even as Christ has forgiven us.

In many cases, anger is actually a symptom of an unmet need. In these situations, anger is actually a secondary response to another primary need. It may be fear, insecurity, or a feeling of being out of control. In these situations, we may feel that expressing our anger and outrage is a way of regaining control.

One of the hardest things about conflict resolution—both for the individual and the professional counselor—is getting in touch with the unmet needs in our lives. We tend to bury and sublimate our drives and motivations. Because we have been trained by years of experience to hide the sources of our irritation, many of us simply cannot get down to the hidden causes of anger and bitterness.

But the positive side of conflict is that it provides an opportunity for growth. When we confront the source of conflict and deal with it head on, we often discover other problems and emotional issues in the background. Dealing with those issues will give us an excellent opportunity to grow emotionally and spiritually.

On the other hand, if we do not deal with the conflict, it will hinder growth; it certainly hinders a satisfying relationship with the other person, particularly in an intimate relationship such as husband-wife or parent-child.

Many of us grew up in homes where we were taught that if we displayed our anger, there would be a serious price to pay. For one thing, the other person might clobber us; but even more dangerous, the other person might withhold affection or even hate us afterward.

Perhaps you grew up in a home where your parents turned off the affection for a while if you got angry. Consequently, you learned to feel that you could not get angry because the other person would withdraw from you or cut you off emotionally. Children desperately need their parents' love and affection, so that's a very scary alternative.

I see couples from time to time who are dealing with this problem. Although they are both seething with anger, they are afraid to show it. Both of them grew up in homes where anger was not allowed, so they tiptoe around each other. It's like they're walking on eggs, while the hostility is building inside them. This is a dangerous and volatile situation. If it is not resolved in a responsible, Christian manner, it can utterly destroy a marriage. I recall another situation where the husband grew up in a home where the mother was always protecting the father. The father was very paternalistic, and the mother always told the kids they must not disturb him with their doubts, their disappointments, their anger, or any overt emotion. She would say, "Shhhh! That's all right, but don't tell your father. Don't say that to Daddy. You know what he will do!"

So this man grew up afraid to confront anyone, no matter how outrageous the person's behavior, because the idea was given to this man by his mother that if he confronted anyone, he would be in deep trouble.

How can anyone deal with everyday life with such a handicap? It certainly is very difficult to overcome that kind of programming, and it generally takes professional help. Fortunately this man is now on his way to recovery, but it is not an easy process for him or the counselor.

How do we deal with situations when we are angry? Let's say we have an unmet need (or at least a perceived unmet need) and we want to get the issue resolved, but we also care deeply about the other person. What's the solution?

In those cases, we often find ourselves in a double bind. "I'm scared of losing you, but I've also got my own integrity to maintain." That's where it really gets sticky.

At the beginning of this chapter, we read some passages from Colossians that talked about some of the responsibilities we have as believers. That seems to be the best place to approach these issues.

Several of the Scripture passages we have discussed so far give us some rather interesting principles about our responsibility as Christians as we try to resolve conflicts with each other. In chapter 4 we read that "a soft answer turns away wrath, but a harsh word stirs up anger."

We know psychologically that it is not wise to deny anger or to suppress it unreasonably. When we are angry with somebody, we need to learn to express our feelings without destroying the other person.

Conflicts are inevitable; we will get angry from time to time. If we live with other people, we will have unmet needs and feel hurt, neglected, and unimportant, and all the other kinds of feelings. At those times, how do we speak the truth in love?

Four Stances in Dealing with Anger
If we don't know how to deal with our conflicts, see them as opportunities for growth, and learn how to speak the truth in love, our conflicts often do just the opposite: they spread poison and discontent that can be self-destructive and can destroy others around us.

Given that situation, we need to think in terms of having some kind of stance when we get into a confrontation. That means that whenever we're dealing with another person and we recognize the potential for disagreement, we should have an attitude of negotiation and compromise to help us avoid a dangerous dispute.

In such a situation, I find that people naturally assume one of four basic stances. The one you choose may determine how successful you will be at conflict resolution.

Again, a diagram may be the best way to describe the steps in this process. We can begin with a horizontal line, which will represent our concern for "the issue." On the far left is total disinterest. At this extreme, we really don't care much about the issue; it's not that big a deal to us. At the opposite extreme is passionate interest in the issue or the subject about which we are in conflict.

WIN / LOSE DIAGRAM

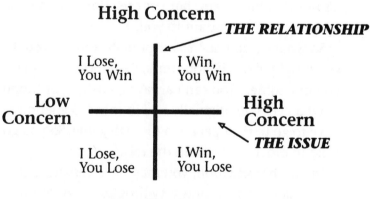

The vertical line represents concern, or lack of concern, for "the relationship." At the top is high, serious concern for the relationship; at the bottom is low concern for the relationship and low regard for the personal consequences involved. The intersection of these two lines creates four quadrants that may be helpful as you begin to consider these ideas.

If you are having a disagreement with another person—whether it is a spouse, a sweetheart, a child, or a peer at work—and if you care very much about the relationship, you probably want that relationship to remain strong and grow through the problem.

When the relationship comes first, the issues will take second place. We can describe our stance in that case as "I Lose, You Win."

Why? Because I care about maintaining the relationship, I take the position that you can have your way; I will not fight you on it. Just think of how many times you've been in that situation. Your wife or husband wants to go to a certain place or do a certain thing, and it's not that important, but your relationship to your spouse is very important to you.

So what do you do? You capitulate and go. You don't get uptight about it. You think, "Well, you win some and you lose some." You can't always go fishing or shopping, or whatever you originally had in mind. Sometimes you have to go to the opera or a football game. So you go. You yield in order to maintain the relationship.

In another situation, you may have very little concern for the issue at stake and very little concern for the relationship. In that case there's hardly any conflict anyway. So you say, in effect, "I don't care about this issue, and I don't care about you, either. So, get lost. I simply don't have the energy to give to this matter, and I don't care what you do about it."

As we see in the lower left quadrant, this is the "I Lose, You Lose" situation.

In the lower right quadrant, I really am concerned

about the issue but I don't care very much about the relationship. That's an "I Win, You Lose" situation.

Compare this attitude to the world of international politics. Think about our delegates to the United Nations as they consider all the various measures that arise. By necessity, they have the attitude, "I really don't care about the other nations of the world. I want what's good for my country. I have great concern about this issue, so, one way or the other, I'm going to win." This is the arena of what I would call *naked power*.

In this quadrant, we assume the position that "I'll take whatever I have to take and do whatever I have to do to win." That is our public stance. The issue is the ultimate thing, and if I have to destroy someone else to get the issue resolved in my favor, tough darts!

The situation that believers have to deal with most often, particularly in our families, jobs, or marriages (which are often the toughest places), is the area in which we care deeply about the issue and we also care deeply about the relationship. This is the "I Win, You Win" quadrant.

This is difficult for a person because he/she wants to maintain the relationship, but also cares very much about this issue. This is the one that takes the most skill, and it is the toughest one in which to control our anger.

Stop, Look, Listen!

How do we learn to package what we say so that the other person has half a chance of hearing us? And even if we present the best package, that will not guarantee that the other person will hear what we are saying.

There's another side to every conflict, and that is the person on the other end. We often feel that our perception is the right one and the other person is confused—he or she has just misperceived or misconstrued the facts.

But there is a further complication: emotions rarely give way to facts. If somebody's hot at you and you think you're going to cool them down with the facts, good luck! It simply does not work that way.

So if I'm on the receiving end, part of my discipline is to learn to be swift to hear and slow to speak, to shut my mouth and try to hear the other person. Then again, the writer of Proverbs said, "Don't talk so much. You keep putting your foot in your mouth. Be sensible and turn off the flow!" (Proverbs 10:19, TLB).

We are so quick to spend our energy and words in our defense that we don't hear the other person. But if I'm angry with you, one of my responsibilities is to try to speak to you about my anger in a way that gives you a chance to hear it. Or if you say something that immediately infuriates me, I should try to respond to you in such a way that you have a chance to see my point of view.

If I am listening to you and you're angry with me, I have a responsibility to try to really hear you and to hear you out before I respond. I should not be spending all my energy working on my defense speech, I need to listen. That is a reasoned and biblical approach, though I assure you it's a lot easier to teach than to practice.

One of the problems in marriage is that of taking each other for granted. Do you ever feel unappreciated by your kids? Do you ever feel like you're running a taxicab service or a bank?

Kids—particularly teenagers—often seem to take our services for granted, and that is frustrating. Somebody said the whole problem of parenting teenagers is that parents want information and control, while kids want money and freedom. Those are diametrically opposed.

When I feel unappreciated, I feel unsupported. That doesn't mean that Jan lies awake at night thinking up creative ways to be unappreciative and unsupportive. It has nothing to do with her intentions. It has to do with what I'm feeling.

The subtleties of what goes on between men and women (or men and men, or women and women, for that matter) are remarkable. For example, one day I decided that I would surprise Jan and clean the house. So I cleaned the house from top to bottom, and I thought, "Oh, I'm going to be so appreciated. And she's going to be so grateful she's got this sensitive, loving, caring husband who just did this nice thing for her."

I had every good intention. I wanted to do it as an expression of love for her. But to my enormous surprise and chagrin, when Jan saw what I had done, she was furious with me.

I couldn't believe it! I did this wonderful thing and she said I was a jerk and an insensitive oaf. So, what did she see? As opposed to what I intended, Jan saw my house-cleaning as a statement that I was critical of her house-keeping ability.

It was as if I had said, "Here, Jan, I'll show you how it should be done!" Now when I realized that was her feeling, it just blew my mind. How could anybody take such a noble, wonderful gesture on my part and interpret it to mean I didn't like how she cleaned the house?

I wanted appreciation, but I got rage and hostility. Amazing! So what was my reaction? I felt unappreciated, so I immediately withdrew. *Well, OK for you,* I thought. *I'll just exclude you from my brilliant company for a while.*

The Battle of Pride

What silly things we do to each other for the sake of pride! If we had had the skills at that time, Jan could have said, "I'm really angry with you, Jim, because I feel that you don't think I am a good housekeeper." And I could have said, "Jan, I believe you are a wonderful house-keeper, but I wanted to please you." If we had done that, we would have cleared up the disagreement right away. But we didn't have the skills, so instead we got into an unfortunate (and memorable) disagreement.

The point of that story is that we need to let people know how we feel. Anger is not a reasonable solution; hostility won't work. Stalking off in a huff won't do it either. We have to back off, process, and talk about it.

It would have been one thing if Jan had kept the house like a pigpen, but she didn't. Jan has always been an immaculate housekeeper. In fact, she's a little too perfectionistic for my taste! I tend to prefer the lived-in look. I sometimes tease Jan that our living room looks more like the Smith Family Museum than a house where people live.

But in speaking the truth in love, as the Bible admonishes, we first have to process our emotions. We try to get in touch with why we're angry, and then we set a time to talk about it. You recall, that was the commit-ment David and Vera Mace made to each other. It's a very practical and wholesome approach to anger that will reduce the pain and hurt.

Unless your relationship is such that you are lying awake at night trying to think up creative ways to irritate someone—your children, your boss, a coworker, or your spouse—you probably want to know when you've done something to hurt or offend another person, particularly if it wasn't intentional. But you need to discover it in a way that you can deal with, don't you? That's when the time-buying statements we discussed in chapter 4 come in handy.

The key to effective conflict resolution is to identify

and clarify the problem. So often we assume that everybody agrees on the core issue when, in fact, there may be total disagreement.

When you get down to the heart of a conflict, especially between husbands and wives, the two people may be in very basic disagreement about what the core issues really are.

Emotional conflict involves how I feel about something, and since we are all unique, there is almost always more than one core issue at stake: your core issue and the other person's core issue. In fact, the issue is usually much more subtle and deeper than the conflict.

If you don't get to the actual core issue, you won't have a ghost of a chance of getting the conflict resolved. There is always the risk that even if you get to the core issue, you may not get it resolved. But if you don't get to the core issue, you *won't* be able to solve it.

In counseling, I find that one of my most difficult tasks is to help people get down to the core issues. It is shocking how often people immediately think divorce when the source of their disappointment and anger has never actually come out into the open.

Toothpaste Wars

People often give the strangest reasons for divorce. For one couple, the reason the woman gave for her anger was that her husband kept squeezing the toothpaste in the middle of the tube after she insisted that it had to be rolled up neatly from the end. These people were ready to split over a tube of toothpaste.

How smart do you have to be to know that the obvious solution to that problem is to buy two tubes of toothpaste? His and hers. But of course, that wasn't the real issue. It was only a symptom of their anger and disappointment.

Our objective has to be to get beneath the surface junk, to dig down to the real source of conflict. So, what do you think the real issue was behind the toothpaste wars? I discovered that this woman came from a very frugal background. She could not bear the idea of wasting toothpaste. When her husband grabbed the tube and clomped down on it, he wasn't worried whether he might be wasting toothpaste; his idea was to brush his teeth, not to conserve toothpaste.

So what else was at issue? It might have been control, but was that all? Every time she came and saw the toothpaste squashed in the middle, leaving stuff down at the bottom that would probably never work its way out, she choked up with anger. This woman had a deep need to be frugal, and she felt her husband squeezed the tube the way he did precisely because he knew it rubbed her the wrong way.

So, what needed to happen? She needed to say, "Honey, it is important to me that we save on toothpaste, and every time I see the toothpaste squeezed in the middle, I feel that you don't think I'm important enough for you to make the effort to care about my concerns. I feel that you don't care about me."

Aha! Suddenly we have discovered the real issue. "I feel that you don't care about me." That is the core issue. For this woman, her husband's behavior was a slap in the face. She said, "I told you a thousand times how important it is to me that you squeeze it from the bottom. You know I get uptight and anxious, and what do you do? I come in and you've clomped it in the middle again, which means you obviously don't care about me."

Emotions rarely submit to facts. If we don't make it

clear that this woman is feeling unimportant, then we don't have much hope of getting the conflict resolved. She won't even be motivated to try.

If he realizes that one of the ways he can say to his wife "You are important to me and I care about you" is to do this little thing that matters to her, then that should be such an easy sacrifice. *It* doesn't have to be important to him, but *she* is. She is his wife, his life partner, his lover and friend. He can either learn how to squeeze toothpaste from the bottom, get his own private tube, or negotiate another solution. The important thing is that he acknowledge his wife's feelings and assure her that he wants to find an agreeable solution. Resolving conflicts through love and concern gives a whole new dimension to the relationship. When we respond in love, not for our own sakes but for the sake of the one we care about, all the subtleties of communication that might otherwise generate conflict can be dealt with.

Financial Responsibilities

Since money problems underlie so many areas of conflict in marriage, perhaps this section will offer a natural transition between our discussion of conflict resolution and the rest of the book.

Over the years, I've had women come to see me because they're having conflict with their husbands over finances. The man may be carrying money to the bank in wheelbarrows, but his wife has no idea where they stand.

Often in those situations the man is trying to maintain a certain image. He wants to be able to say, "Honey, just buy whatever you need. I'll worry about the money." So she does, but when he gets the bills he goes through the roof.

Well, that's not fair! If he wants to keep his wife in the

dark, he can't blame her for spending blindly. Regardless of who the primary money manager is, both partners ought to know how the family is doing, what the budget limits are, and how the husband and wife, together, can cooperate to keep the household accounts in proper balance. And they should construct the budget together.

If the husband is the primary money manager, he can say, "Honey, you can spend $1,000 ($5,000, $10,000—whatever the budget allows) on clothes, and that's it." Then if she spends $500, there's no reason to complain. But if he chooses to keep her in the dark and she goes over the budget, that's a problem that he created.

Many times wives are left with a lot of tension about finances because they don't have all the information and don't know the facts. At our house, Jan and I do the books together. I'm not sure how we got started doing it that way, but it has been a wonderful way of keeping us both on the same page.

Jan writes the checks when I'm not around, but normally I pay the bills. I have no objection if she does it, but we have a system, and part of the system is that I keep a single loose-leaf notebook that I update every year. In that notebook is everything Jan needs to know in the event anything should happen to me.

The notebook has complete information about our insurance policies. It has a list of attorneys, a list of bank accounts, and a complete record of everything she would need to know, all in one place.

Once a year we go over that information together. We take a look at our estate (as small as it may be) so that whatever happens, Jan is not going to have a lot of anxiety wondering who to contact or what to do to get our finances in order. Even if I am primarily responsible for maintaining our household records, she needs to be just as informed about all those things as I am.

In many households these days, the wife is the primary money manager. Often, the women are the practical ones. They have a big investment in the family, children, family traditions, and social life, so it is just as natural for her to keep up with the financial matters as for her husband.

Also, men who spend all day in the workplace dealing with budgets, balances, and figures of one kind or another don't necessarily want to have to come home and do the same thing all night. They are glad when their wives offer to handle the family finances.

However you do it at your house, it should be a household rule that you both take an active interest in your finances, sharing the responsibility for maintaining budgets, and knowing where and how your records are maintained.

The system Jan and I use helps us deal with some of the stresses of financial pressure and financial difficulty. Since both Jan and I work, we have found it convenient to keep two checking accounts. In every household, unless one of you is an absolute idiot with money (and I understand that occasionally that is the case!), I think the two checking account routine is a good idea. A woman ought to have her own account, and a man ought to have his.

In addition, I often suggest there should be a place for funds designated as "fun money." Every month Jan and I each get a certain amount for fun money, and neither of us is accountable to the other for how we spend it.

Most of the time I don't even know what Jan does with her fun money. She may be playing the horses, for all I know. I never ask, nor do I feel I should. But we each have a certain amount of discretionary funds that we can use as we please.

One of the worst things a husband can do is to arrange the finances so that his wife feels she always has to come to him to ask for money. That is demeaning, as if the woman of the house were on a par with the children.

While I handle most of the banking and investments in our family, Jan handles most of the household accounts. What she spends for food and clothes and the like comes out of a general account while the things she buys for herself come primarily from her own funds.

Jan doesn't have to account to me for what she buys just as I don't have to account to her for the things I buy. While we both have to live within the family budgets, we are also both responsible adults.

So if she comes home with something outlandish, and if I say, "Where on earth did that monstrosity come from?" she can say (and she does!), "Fun money." That's the end of it.

On the other hand, If I come home with a new gun, or a new hunting dog, I just say, "Fun money!" before she asks. You have to be honest about it, obviously, but knowing you have your own discretionary funds helps to take some of the pressure off the whole business of finances.

The Four Emotional Needs

Basically, people have four emotional needs. They can all start with the letter *A*, if you like. That is a helpful way to remember them. First of all, people need *affection*, feeling that they are special to someone else; they need *acceptance*, a sense of belonging; they need *affirmation*, being told they have significance; and they need *agreement*, which is not obedience or subservience, but a sense of common goals, shared beliefs, and mutuality.

In short, we all need to be loved, we need to feel we contribute significantly, that we're accepted, and that we're in this thing together. Those are the foundation blocks of a healthy Christian marriage.

Our basic psychological needs aren't very complex. They are not difficult to meet if we have healthy relationships. But we all need to have at least one relationship that sustains us, encourages us, and gives us a basic sense of worth.

In a healthy marriage we must learn that at least 50 percent of our job is to provide that sort of encouragement and care for our spouse. It is not enough to take our own dividends out of the marriage investment if we are not also paying back into the fund.

When we strive to identify and resolve the conflicts that will inevitably arise in marriage, and when we seek to affirm and support our partner, we will discover the true joy of the relationship. We will also come that much closer to understanding the blessing that God meant marriage to be.

EIGHT

WHAT EVERY WOMAN WANTS

In the next two chapters, we want to talk about some of the unique distinctions between husband and wife, male and female, man and woman. While in the preceding chapters we have been dealing with some of the broader issues, I now want to be more specific.

So far we have talked about communication and conflict in marriage. We have looked at some of the characteristics of healthy marriages and some of the threats. Now I want to look at the individuals themselves.

As we begin, let's look at a very familiar passage of Scripture. If you have ever read anything on marriage from a Christian perspective, you have read this one:

> You wives must submit to your husbands' leadership in the same way you submit to the Lord. For a husband is in charge of his wife in the same way Christ is in charge of his body the Church. (He gave his very life to take care of it and be its Savior!) So you wives must willingly obey your husbands in everything, just as the Church obeys Christ.
>
> And you husbands, show the same kind of love to

your wives as Christ showed to the Church when he
died for her, to make her holy and clean, washed by
baptism and God's Word; so that he could give her
to himself as a glorious Church without a single spot
or wrinkle or any other blemish, being holy and
without a single fault. (Ephesians 5:22-27, TLB)

These verses are preceded by verse 21, which says:
"Honor Christ by submitting to each other."

Isn't it interesting that husbands are told to love their
wives, but wives are never told to love their husbands? I
don't want to get into a discussion as to why I believe
Paul expressed it that way, but it is a clear commandment
that husbands are to love their wives as they love their
own bodies.

I interpret that to mean that a husband is to learn to
love his wife with great sensitivity and caring; to learn to
meet her needs just as he would want his own needs met.

In a sense, it is like the *Golden Rule of Marriage,* isn't it?
Paul is commanding husbands to do unto their wives as
they would want their wives to do unto them, and certainly as they would do unto themselves; that is, whether
or not their wives do unto them!

Physiological Differences
I don't know if you have ever noticed, but men and
women are attuned to their bodies in very different ways.
When a man is hungry, he wants to eat when? An hour
ago. Right? If he's feeling passionate, he wants to fulfill
that need when? Immediately!

I believe women have a deeper, more intuitive understanding of physiology and health. They know about
their biology, they understand cycles and timing, and
how nutrition works. They know why it is important to

maintain a healthy body, and they are very much in touch with their physical needs and in planning how to meet those needs. I believe women are blessed with a natural understanding of these things.

Unfortunately, most men could care less about physiology or biology when it comes to their own bodies. Cycles and nutrition and proper planning are as foreign to most of them as the moons of Jupiter. But they know what they want. They know when they want it, and they generally know how to get it.

So, if we consider the natural behavior of men and women, some paradoxes and difficulties will certainly arise. We have already said that, "in the wild," men and women are very different and potentially destructive to each other. I would like to focus on what it means for men to be sensitive to the needs of their wives. In the following chapter, we will explore the other side of the equation: the needs of men.

In every healthy marriage there has to be an ongoing concern for the comfort and well-being of both partners. Both need to have a sense of what the other is feeling, what he or she is dealing with, and how they are faring emotionally.

As an experiment, take a piece of paper and pencil and work through it with me. I am using the "ten common sources of depression in women" originally cited in Dr. James Dobson's book *What Wives Wish Their Husbands Knew about Women* (Tyndale House, 1977). There may well be other concerns not on this list, but these are fairly common. And since this list was used in a national survey, I think it will provide a suitable example.

When I give this exercise in a class situation, normally I ask the men to rank, from 1 to 10, how they feel their wives would rate the various items on the list. If they're not married, I ask them to think in terms of their fiancée, girlfriend, or other woman friend.

If a man feels that the number one cause of frustration and depression in his wife (or friend) is "aging," then he should put a 1 at that spot on the list. If he feels that "in-law conflict" is the second greatest source of depression in her life, he should put a 2 by that one.

Women should do the same thing, except that they should rank the items from their own perspective. These should be the things that they find most depressing in their own lives.

It is safe to assume that the women will be more attuned to what causes greater depression in their own lives than their husbands or boyfriends, but that may or may not be the case. At any rate, take a minute now and complete your list.

    Common Sources of Depression in Women
      1. Absence of romantic love
      2. In-law conflict
      3. Low self-esteem
      4. Problems with the kids
      5. Financial difficulties
      6. Loneliness, isolation, and boredom
      7. Sexual problems
      8. Menstrual or physiological problems
      9. Fatigue and time pressure
    10. Aging

When I give this exercise to groups of men and women, the results are always interesting. We recognize that, by and large, men aren't always in touch with their own emotions, but they are often surprisingly well in touch with what causes depression in their wives. That may be a defense mechanism. Who knows? But the men's list and the women's list do differ in some ways.

On the women's list, "fatigue and time pressure" frequently ranks number 1, and there is a tie for second place between "absence of romantic love" and "loneliness, isolation, and boredom." But number 3 is characteristically "financial difficulties," and number 4 is "low self-esteem."

The men who have taken the survey in groups that I have taught usually think that there is a two-way tie for the number 1 spot between "absence of romantic love" and "low self-esteem." They think that "fatigue and time pressure" is number 2, that "loneliness, isolation, and boredom" is number 3, and that number 4 is "financial difficulties." Even though the order is slightly different, the men isolate the same basic areas as being areas of pressure for their wives.

In the national survey cited by Dr. Dobson, researchers came up with similar results. In this survey, conducted among women aged twenty-five to forty, all professing to be Christians, "low self-esteem" was reportedly the number one cause of depression among women. Number 2 was "fatigue and time pressure."

At that point, there was a two-way tie for third between "loneliness, isolation, and boredom," and "absence of romantic love." I suspect those things are really very much related. Number 4 in the national survey was "financial difficulties."

Having isolated a half dozen areas of concern in the lives of women, I would like to discuss these in more detail, beginning with the area most often ranked at the top of the women's list: fatigue and time pressure.

The fact that this category is on the list and that it

ranks consistently high is an interesting commentary on our country. We are people on the go.

Dallas, where I live and work, is a classic example of life in the very, very fast lane. So many women I meet feel they're running a motel and a taxicab service. That can be such a drag, and no wonder it causes depression in women.

Life in the Fast Lane

It seems to me that if a Christian husband wanted to love his wife as Christ loved the church, and to promote a healthy marriage, he would want to relieve her of this pervasive source of depression in her life. If his wife is saying, "I'm suffering because of all the fatigue and time pressure I feel," then he should consider some of the following options.

First, husband and wife should *take a close look at each other's schedules.* I would say they should take a ruthless look! It takes an enormous amount of courage to get your sanity back if you live in a busy American city these days.

Jan and I try to do a time inventory once a year. We look at the things we've gotten ourselves into and we try to decide whether or not we want to continue doing all those things. We find that we have to weed out some of them. So many things have gotten into our schedules, we have to take a cold look at our values, priorities, commitments, and personal needs. Then we chop everything that doesn't fit.

As I said earlier, one time Jan and I concluded that we were going to so many Christian meetings we didn't have time to be Christian. That was the year we gave up going to Christian meetings for Lent!

As it turned out, there was a certain amount of guilt over that decision. A lot of people feel that being spiritual demands going to Christian meetings. But Jan and I have discovered since that time that if we do not block out time for each other, we simply don't get it.

That brings us to the second point—*set aside time for each other.* If you wait to see what sort of time is left for your spouse at the end of your busy day, or at the end of your busy week, that's all you'll get: what's left. That attitude certainly communicates something to your spouse. It may not be what you want to say, but it speaks loudly, believe me. I'm a great believer in planning for time with your spouse before the week begins, and that might mean at the beginning of the year. If you have difficulty with this, you might consider going through your entire calendar during the holidays and blocking out times for each other.

If you don't do something like that, it won't happen. If a husband wants to show his wife that he cares deeply about her, he should invite her to sit down with him and, with calendar in hand, plan their time together. There is no substitute for that kind of strategy session.

I think *quality time* means *a quantity of time.* You cannot have one without the other. When we truly love someone, we want to spend time with that person, and no "quality half hour" can make up for a loving morning or afternoon or weekend together.

Some of you are going to have to quit letting your kids run your schedule. That means that the kids don't always get to do everything they want to do (or perhaps they ought not to be doing everything you think they ought to be doing). If your children are running your schedule, you're in trouble. You may have to tell them there are going to be certain nights of the week that are *your* nights. You may have to set aside your special night when the kids can do without you.

Setting aside these times may be tough for a man who's building his career and is working night and day. But it is also a matter of priorities. What comes first? What will matter at the end when you cash in your chips? Any man who cares for his wife will give her some special time of her own. If it doesn't come easily and naturally, then he may have to schedule it. But it should be her own, uninterrupted time.

Third—and this will probably get me into trouble—*mothers also need some time away from the demands made on them by their children,* especially very young children who demand so much time and attention.

I don't know how to tell you to do that, but it might mean that every week on Thursday night, for example, she gets a night off and the husband takes care of the kids. Thursday is his special night with the children, and, to make it more special, Mom arranges to do something else that night. If she wants to go shopping with her friends or just go somewhere and sit under a tree and collapse, or whatever she wants to do, that is her private time. While she's out, Dad takes responsibility for feeding and bathing the kids and getting them off to bed.

I will guarantee any man that if he does that for his wife, particularly if they have small children, she will love him for it. You may need to redirect some of your income toward making that possible. Fatigue and time pressure will suddenly slide to a much lower spot on her list of complaints.

It takes a lot of courage to get off the treadmill in today's fast-paced culture. But you have to come to the point where you can say, "We're going to stop this nonsense. We're not going to let ourselves get involved in everything that comes down the pike, no matter how good it may seem at the time." You have to make a commitment to save some time for each other, and to slow down the pace. Is it difficult to do? Probably. Is it worth it? No doubt about it.

I have learned to limit my civic responsibilities. I will not commit to more than one civic function or club a year. I will serve on an advisory board if they understand that I will not come to meetings. I will not do more than that because I know where it leads.

People who let themselves fall into that trap spend all their time running from one board meeting to another. Chances are it isn't doing any good and it creates fatigue and time pressure on everyone in the family. Do you believe that you need time together, as well as some time alone, to live sanely? Then don't get hooked on activity for activity's sake.

I see too many wives who let themselves get stuck with too many commitments. They're running twenty-four hours a day with their tongues hanging out. They're running shuttle systems and day-care and pickup-and-delivery to soccer and swimming and band. Sooner or later they meet themselves going around in circles! An overcommitted life creates havoc for a woman, just as it does in the way she relates with her husband.

I suggest to each husband: part of your courtship this week is to say, "Honey, let's sit down and talk about our schedules." And after you whittle down the list of commitments, plan a time for the two of you.

Men, let me tell you something about women. They can live the whole week knowing they've got one night with you if they can have your undivided attention. If a husband takes his wife out to dinner, just the two of them, and he's there physically, but his mind is still at the office or someplace else, that's no good. That's not the plan. It has to be a genuine time of togetherness and sharing. Many women have told me that they can go a long time on the promise of that two or three hours of undivided attention.

Some of the best exercise you can get this week is to stand in front of the mirror and practice saying no. Say "No, no, no!" till it starts to feel natural. How many times do you say yes to someone, for someone else's sake, and actually go away feeling resentful? So why not learn how to say no?

Men and Romance

Among the various causes of depression among women, the number 2 response was a combination of "loneliness, isolation, and boredom," and "absence of romantic love." Let's talk about the most interesting one first: romance.

Generally speaking, women tend to be much more romantic than men. Personally, I have always had to work at being romantic. I grew up in West Virginia, near the coal mines where everything was just dirt practical. Early in my married life, I always thought in practical terms. If it was Jan's birthday, I thought we ought to get something practical. What's practical? Well, if we needed a new sweeper, I would give her a sweeper for her birthday.

That's certainly practical, but it isn't very romantic. It took years for me to realize that what really pleased Jan most was something absolutely impractical, but personal and pretty.

Since we were in the ministry, I thought we should always be very practical. A practical gift was a wonderful way to show Jan how responsible I was being. So, when Christmas or birthdays came around, out came the practical presents! But not anymore.

I have learned that women want something romantic. But what's romantic? Flowers are romantic. Perfume is romantic. Negligees are romantic. If you're too embarrassed, ask someone to help you do the shopping. That's something else men don't do very well: shop!

I will tell you something else I have learned about women. You cannot tell her too many times a day that you love her. I have never had a woman come to me and say, "I've got a horrible problem. My husband will not quit telling me he loves me. He just bores me to tears with it. He tells me incessantly." I do not think that a woman can hear that too much, if it is a genuine expression of affection and love.

An occasional phone call during the day to say, "I was thinking about you. How's your day going?" is romantic. It's relational. Unfortunately, men tend to let that slide as time goes by. They forget the romance in marriage. Also a lot of people's sex lives fall apart because the husband stops being romantic.

Some men need to know that foreplay has more to do with the way they say good-bye in the morning than with their bedroom technique. Romance is such an important part of the marriage relationship for most wives. They may not make a big deal about it, but they love the romance, and they need romance and sincere affection from their mate to feel complete.

Candlelight is romantic. From time to time you might suggest having dinner by candlelight. If she switches off the light and puts out a candle, don't yell, "Hey, I can't see the food!" Don't do something totally unromantic when she's trying to create a mood! Get into the mood with her.

One of the things I encourage young couples to do is to get into the habit of doing little courtship things for each other. Couples don't have to give up the romance just because the honeymoon is over. They should continue the courtship.

Have you ever thought about the difference between the oriental and the western views of marriage? Most Occidentals—that is, Anglo-Saxons and others of European heritage—see marriage as a sort of ritual that involves courtship, falling in love, and eventually marrying the person they love.

The oriental view, on the other hand, at least the traditional view, is that marriages are a sort of business arrangements. Courtship doesn't even start until after the wedding. Once the couple is married, then each person will try to learn to love the person he or she married. It's a very different mind-set.

The tragedy of Western marriages is that most of us quit courting once we're married. That's sad.

Women have told me, "I feel like my husband just takes me for granted. Before we were married, I felt very special. Now it's just business as usual."

When I first began to explore these concepts in my own life, I had to write myself notes. I would take my calendar and think of something romantic that I could do with Jan, and then I would scribble it in where I'd be sure to see it.

I think Jan thought I had undergone some sort of miraculous transformation, but I was really working at it, little by little. I had to have a system because I didn't grow up with it. My father wasn't romantic; my grandfather wasn't romantic. I had never seen it demonstrated, but Jan wanted and expected romance in marriage.

Occasionally, the woman may be very practical and the husband will be the romantic one. That's an interesting switch in roles. Generally speaking, however, the wife is more romantic than the husband, and she needs romance to make her feel close to her husband.

If her husband allows the courtship to end after the wedding, she's going to start to feel lonely, isolated, and bored. That is why we see that category near the top of the list on surveys like the one we have been discussing.

But consider another perspective. Husbands needs to be romanced a little, too, believe it or not. He may not know it, but he likes it.

At a weekend retreat for couples where I spoke several years ago, I asked the group what kind of little romantic things they did for their mates that they found most effective.

One of the fellows said, "Well, my wife packs my lunch every day, and every day she takes a bite out of my sandwich. When lunch break comes, I open it and I see there's a bite missing, and that just lets me know she's kind of thinking of me."

Then he went on to say, "One day we had a real fight before I left for work, and when I opened my lunch box, the whole sandwich was there. No bite was missing, and I knew I was in trouble."

I'm not sure if you would want to try that approach. But if you pack your husband's lunch, you might put a note in it sometime. I told the staff at my church this story a few years. One day when we were having a staff meeting, one of the guys bit into his sandwich and stopped suddenly, opened his sandwich, and there was a note inside.

That was a nice touch, but the only problem was that his wife had written the note with a bleeding pen and it turned his whole tuna fish sandwich bright blue! But we all laughed and applauded the effort. At least there was an attempt to say "Hey, I'm thinking of you."

If you are married, do you still remember what it was like when you were dating? Do you remember the emotions you felt? If you have only been married a short time, you will certainly remember your courtship. You were always looking for some way to say to the other person, "You're special. I'm thinking of you. I care for you."

I don't care if you've been married fifty years, courtship is still an important part of your relationship. I especially enjoy seeing older couples who are visibly in love with each other. I love to see men and women of any age walking down the street together, hand in hand.

Keeping that attitude in a marriage keeps the marriage fresh. If there is an element of love and romance, then we won't start to feel that we're being taken for granted. It's a very important aspect of marriage that many of us tend to forget. But we should continue to court our mates, in one way or the other, for the rest of our lives.

Learning to share what is going on in your work will help your wife not feel lonely, isolated, and bored. In most cases, hearing about your work is not a burden for her. She enjoys it.

I made this big mistake when I was first married. I figured Jan had enough problems of her own, and I sure wasn't going to burden her with mine. Again, I thought I was being really noble, so I didn't share any of my problems with her.

I kept silent about my workday out of a desire to protect Jan from my struggles. It was my way of saying, "Hey, you've got enough strain of your own. Why should I bring home my strain and put it on you?" But what Jan heard was that I was shutting her out of my life.

She knew how important my work was to me. When I chose not to tell her about my work, she began to feel that she must not be very important to me. So I learned that no matter how stressed she seemed, my wife wanted to hear about what was important to me. I needed to make an effort to share with her what was going on in my life.

I keep going back to this, but it's so important! Women like details. You can't just say, "I had a neat day at the office today. Did a lot of good correspondence and made a couple of deals." That won't cut it. She wants more than that.

You'll think, "I don't want to rehash all these problems." But, that's your gift to her. She needs to have a sense of sharing. Healthy marriages work that way, and that means it's going to take some work for both of you.

Husbands need to make a bit of an effort to open up and share what's going on with their work. They have to think in terms of being romantic or of doing something romantic. Those little things can mean so much!

During my career as a counselor, I have discovered over and over again that it is not the great big things that knock a marriage in the head. It's all the little ones. If you want a healthy marriage, you're going to have to work at all the little things. The little tokens. It's amazing how big they can be.

Every day I try to find some way to let Jan know that she's special to me. I find that it means a lot to her, but it means just as much to me. When I think about those things, it makes me realize just how much I treasure our relationship.

Money Matters
Number 3 on the list was financial difficulties. This is a tough one. It's harder because there are so many dynamics to it. Some men feel they have to protect their wives from all the financial realities.

A few years ago, a woman came to see me shortly after her husband died. She had never written a check in her life. She had never paid a bill. When her husband died, she was totally unable to take care of herself financially. She had enough money in the bank, but she had no idea how to use it. Talk about feeling helpless! She was a bright and attractive woman, but all of a sudden she felt absolutely stupid and lost.

In my opinion, that husband was guilty of criminal neglect. In thinking that he was protecting his wife from the harsh realities of life, he was actually forcing a serious handicap upon her.

I'm a great believer in budgets. But I don't care if you make a million dollars a year—and I've counseled plenty of millionaires and multimillionaires, both before and after marriage—setting up and managing a family budget is a shared responsibility. It involves both the husband and the wife.

Building Your Wife's Self-Esteem

Women don't compete with other women the way men compete with other men. That is one reason why women are generally much more clothes conscious than men. When men go to a business meeting or a lunch appointment, I doubt if many of them take a long look around to see how the other guys are dressed. But I have a strong suspicion most women do as a matter of habit. I think that's one reason it takes women longer to get dressed. They're getting ready to go out and compete.

If a man is going to compete with his peers he may say, "Well, do you want to go out on the basketball court and try me one-on-one?" Or he may say, "Okay, let's just compare your deal with my deal." That's the way men compete. It's much more physical, more tangible. Women generally compete with other women based on personal qualities, such as taste, attractiveness, appearance, personal charm, and less over what they *do*. So, of course they are going to spend more money on clothes, makeup, and jewelry. That is part of their battle gear.

Just as wives are sensitive to the competitive natures of their husbands, men need to be sensitive to the competitive traits of their wives. That doesn't mean it has to get out of hand; this can be done reasonably. A new dress may be just as important to her as a new set of golf clubs (or whatever his favorite hobby may be) to him. If every man at the office showed up in the same suit, they might get a good laugh out of it, but nobody would be mortified. If any two women in a room showed up with the same dress, they would both head for the exit, humiliated. For them it would be a global disaster, or worse.

Now her husband might say, "Honey, you look great. You look much better than what's-her-name!" But that isn't what matters to her. She is competing with other women, and that just took the competition out of it. It isn't fair, from her viewpoint, which explains why she is constantly worried about how her hair looks.

Not all of us are in the same financial position. So men, please understand that women may feel very bad about their appearance because they simply can't compete with the same high-quality merchandise. I know women who struggle over coming to church because they are self-conscious that their husband's income is not as great as the other men in the church.

Men, on the other hand, don't worry much about that. If we all had to bring our Dun and Bradstreet statements to get a seat, we might have some serious doubts. But the fact that the guy next to me makes three or four times what I make is no big deal. Still, we need to be sensitive to each other's needs, and to the basic emotions and motivations of our spouses.

We have already discussed the importance of self-esteem. It is not surprising that it ranks high on this list as a cause of depression in women. How important is it that husbands work on their wives' self-esteem? We should know by now that it is very, very important. Every husband worth his salt should know that he is the number one source of his wife's self-esteem.

I hope all men learn that truth. If the way we behave toward our wife determines her emotional attitude, and if what we say to her helps to shape her inner sense of worth, shouldn't we strive to build her up and praise her for all she does? I certainly believe so. I think it's a biblical mandate.

Most men need to learn some social graces. If you take your wife out to dinner and some voluptuous blonde shimmies by while you are sitting there and your wife loses you for twenty minutes, you don't have to say a thing. You have already said enough! Sitting there all glassy-eyed with your mouth hanging open isn't doing much for your wife's self-esteem.

It is important to show respect for your wife and to tell her when you find her attractive. Tell her when you like the way she's dressed. Self-esteem and romance in the marriage are very close to each other at this point, and we have already seen that they both rank very high on a woman's scale of felt needs.

I am not suggesting that a husband should be phony or syrupy when he compliments his wife. That's not necessary; she will spot it in a minute. Get in the habit of looking at her from time to time, observe what she's wearing. She works hard to be attractive, mostly for your sake, so take notice and tell her you like the way she looks. Is that too much?

We find it easy to tear down the other person's self-esteem; so why can't we build it up instead? When your wife does something well, compliment her. Don't take her cooking or housekeeping or child-rearing or job skills for granted. Let her know you appreciate the time she spends doing all the difficult tasks she does for you and the kids.

One of the great sins that people fall into—and it works both ways—is that we are guilty of not appreciating each other. The sin of *unappreciation:* that may not be correct English, but it makes the point.

We need to learn to express and show our appreciation for each other. If a man will start letting his wife know what he appreciates, and if he tells her daily, he will see her energy level rise. We all need that, and it means so much to a woman!

I tell husbands to thank their wives for as many legitimate things as they can think of. Let them know what you like about them, and when they do things especially well. Don't keep it a secret; let them know that you notice and you care. The older women get, the more important this is to them.

When you think about what women in America today are up against, as far as what our culture has said to them, you realize what an incredible strain they are under. On top of that, we seem to be saying, as a society, that the greatest sin in America today is "growing old." American culture places so much emphasis on youth and beauty and fitness. Women can no longer grow old gracefully as our mothers and grandmothers were allowed to do. We don't even have the same standards of aging for men in our culture. Older men seem to get a lot more respect than older women. Why should that be true? Again, our standards are out of balance. It's up to Christians to help bring back a bit of sanity and respect.

Every woman is going to grow older; but because she understands how the system works, that's really scary to her. Maybe she understands what Erma Bombeck realized when she wrote, "I've got everything I had twenty years ago, it's all just four inches lower!"

Acting Your Age

It is important that we show greater love and affection for women as they begin to mature. There are so many things a woman only learns by growing older. But the emphasis of our culture seems to be on the cute, young chicks.

Women see the fifty-year-old men taking up with twenty-five-year-old women, and that can be threatening. But that says something about men, too, doesn't it? It's not very flattering, but it does say something.

As we age together, we ought to be able to find new ways to stroke and encourage our wife. We must learn to show respect, affection, and love for our wife. If we do succeed in building her self-esteem, we'll get it back sevenfold.

The man who treats his wife like a queen will be treated like a king. It's just the way God made women to respond. So let me encourage every husband, or husband-to-be, to think about some of these things. Do them now, and do them often. You may have to work at it in the beginning. A lot of men find it difficult to express their emotions. But in time it will become much easier and much more natural. Soon you will realize that you do esteem her, just as you say.

I had to learn all of these things from scratch. And I

had to learn some of them the hard way. But my relationship with my wife has grown stronger every day. And my own sense of self-esteem (not pride, but self-esteem) has grown right along with it!

But now let's take a look at some of the things a woman can do for her husband.

NINE

WHAT EVERY MAN WANTS

The passage of Scripture we read in Ephesians 5 has been interpreted as a statement that a husband is to love his wife with great sensitivity to her needs:

> That is how husbands should treat their wives, loving them as parts of themselves. For since a man and his wife are now one, a man is really doing himself a favor and loving himself when he loves his wife! No one hates his own body but lovingly cares for it. (Ephesians 5:28-30, TLB)

In exploring the needs of women, we talked about what men need to know about their wives, and we saw that the husband's scriptural responsibility is to love and care for his wife. Now it's only fair that we look at the other side: that is, what women need to know about men. To keep things in a similar vein, I would like to use a list of "ten common sources of depression in men" (call it irritation or melancholy if you prefer), similar to the women's list we used in the last chapter.

On a sheet of paper, women should make a list of the

problems, in order of importance, that they think are the greatest irritants and causes of depression in their husbands, boyfriends, or other male friends. Men will want to list them from most irritating to least irritating, as they feel them in their own lives.

I hope that husbands and wives, engaged couples, or anyone who wants to understand the dynamics of a healthy male-female relationship will try this exercise. Compare notes with your spouse or friend of the opposite sex on what these lists turn up.

Looking at what each of you thought about the women's list and then the men's list will help you both better understand where each person is coming from. It's important that you compare how you perceive things compared to how your partner perceives them. That can be a surprising experience in itself.

In some cases, husbands and wives are very much in tune with each other's feelings and attitudes; in other cases, they need to try to get in tune. An exercise like this can be a wonderful tool for dialogue and for bringing greater understanding and empathy in a relationship.

One of the marvelous things about Scripture is that it puts our focus where it belongs. Most troubled marriages are characterized by two people standing across the room shouting at each other, "I want *my* needs met—now!" But the Bible tells us that in a healthy marriage, the husband is to focus on the wife's needs and the wife is to focus on the husband's needs.

When both do that, guess what happens? Needs get met. Rather than demanding that his own needs be met, the husband realizes that his Christian commitment and responsibility is to focus on his wife and her needs. The wife, in turn, realizes that her commitment is to focus on her husband's needs. It may not always work out perfectly—temperaments vary a great deal—but when both sets of needs are being met, basically there is a healthy marriage.

Common Sources of Depression in Men
1. Fear of failure in business
2. Fear of loss of job
3. Low self-esteem
4. Fear of loss of masculinity
5. Financial difficulties
6. Inability to attain occupational goals
7. Sexual problems
8. Fatigue and time pressure
9. Problems with the kids
10. Aging

In the classes I have taught on this topic, most of the women felt that their husbands would say the number 1 cause of depression, melancholy, or irritation in their life is "fatigue and time pressure." They thought the number 2 factor is "fear of failure in business," and that number 3 is "inability to attain occupational goals."

Number 4 on the women's list has generally been "financial difficulties," while "low self-esteem" comes in somewhere around number 5.

On the men's list, the number 1 concern has generally been a tie between "fatigue and time pressure" and "fear of failure in business." Again, wives and husbands in these groups were, to my surprise, very much in tune on these concerns. The men felt that "financial difficulties" was the number 2 cause of melancholy, and number 3 was "inability to attain occupational goals." They also felt that "low self-esteem" ranked fourth or fifth down the list.

Unfortunately, there is no national comparison for this

list, but it is astonishing how uniformly the husbands and wives seemed to be pinpointing the same issues, both on the husbands' and the wives' concerns. It hasn't always been that way; in fact, we would normally expect the opinions of husbands and wives to be greatly at odds on such subjects. Perhaps the growing concern over the institution of marriage has made us all more sensitive to each other's needs and emotions. I hope so.

Now, it becomes especially interesting when we compare the top causes of depression and irritation between the responses to the women's list in the last chapter and the men's list above.

WOMEN'S CONCERNS	MEN'S CONCERNS
1. Low self-esteem	1a. Fatigue and time pressure
2. Fatigue and time pressure	1b. Fear of failure in business
3a. Loneliness, isolation, and boredom	2. Financial difficulties
3b. Absence of romantic love	3. Inability to attain occupational goals
4. Financial difficulties	4. Low self-esteem

One of the things this comparison tells us about the basic differences between men and women is that men tend to be wrapped up in their work and get most of their strokes about who they are from their work. Women, on the other hand, are more concerned about what's going on in the marriage and the home. They are much more sensitive to what's happening with the children than the men are; but they are even more sensitive to what's happening in their husbands' lives.

One of the obvious implications of these findings is that husbands need to recognize how their life and work affect their wives. When a man shuts his wife out of his business concerns and his work, she feels shut out of his life. She realizes what an important factor his job is for him. That's why it is so important that he talk to her about his life in detail. She needs to hear specifics. But, let's look at the men's top concerns, beginning with fatigue and time pressure.

Fighting the Clock

Do you sometimes get the feeling that maybe we're living at a much faster pace than God ever intended? I really believe that.

If you have traveled abroad or spent any time at all in a foreign country, you know what a peculiar feeling it can be to come back to America. Whenever I have been overseas for a while and have come back to the States, I feel like I'm trying to step on a merry-go-round that somebody has cranked up to full tilt!

Sometimes I get this feeling just coming home from vacation. Jan and I spent ten days in New Mexico last year, very relaxed, trekking around in the wilderness. But the minute we got back—just being on the freeway driving home from the airport—we could immediately feel our anxiety levels starting to rise. Getting back to life in the fast lane was enough to raise our blood pressure about six notches.

I remember how different it felt spending a week pheasant hunting on a ranch near MacDonald, Kansas. MacDonald is not the end of the world, but you can actually see it from there. It is a town of about 309 people, and the contrast between life there and in Dallas, where I live, is absolutely startling.

It doesn't take long to fall into the slow, comfortable, easygoing way of life in a place like that. But when you come back home and get into whatever you do in the city, the rat race starts all over again, at a frantic pace.

We know that we need to put on the brakes; we know we'll live longer if we do. But with all the pressure on us in today's culture, it takes a lot of courage to slow our life-styles down and not get sucked into the whirlwind. We know that the fast life just chews people up and spits them out, but we keep going back for more. Why?

Time for Decompression
Let me suggest a couple of things for wives, particularly for those who have primarily chosen the vocation of being a full-time homemaker. If you have chosen a career in the home, you can give your husband a wonderful gift every night. It is known as *decompression time.*

It is difficult for most men to shift their gears quickly from the business world to the family world. They need some time to cycle down when they're coming out of the knock-down-drag-out work world back to their family world.

I call it decompression time because the term, which comes from scuba diving, seems so apt. If you have ever done any scuba diving, or even if you have just seen one of those Jacques Cousteau documentaries, you probably know that if divers come up too quickly, they get the bends. So, divers come up gradually to allow the oxygen level in their blood to adjust to the changing environ-ment.

Your husband may just want to sit and gaze into space for half an hour. He may just go glassy-eyed; a zombie. He may want to read the afternoon newspaper (perhaps the sports section, since anything else these days just cre-ates more tension).

Your commitment is to give him that time. It is your

gift to him. But his commitment, then, is that after you and the children have given him a little time to chill out, he rejoins the family. He cannot just sit there the rest of the evening, glazed over, watching the television; that's not fair to anybody.

Providing a little space for him to cool off can be an enormous gift to a husband. But the couple needs to talk about it and agree on what they're doing, and why they're doing it. Make sure your husband knows that you will give him this time because you love him. But I will be so bold as to offer a warning as well. If you do not agree to some kind of decompression period, chances are that your husband will find a way to do it on his own terms. If he's typical of most men, that's the way he's made.

Driving home from work in heavy traffic is not a time to cycle down, so some men choose to hang around the office for a while to get organized and clear out the fog. Others may simply go into slow motion to avoid coming home; while still others may be tempted to stop off at a bar on the way home where there are few demands, where the bartender is a good listener, and where he can have the illusion of relaxing.

There is no doubt that "happy hour" is a dangerous alternative, not only to a husband or wife but to the entire family; yet it has become a very common one for many these days. Many men fell into that habit when they were looking for a way to "relax."

Of course, there are other alternatives for cooling down, some of them quite natural. A man in one of my classes lived for a period of time about five miles from Puget Sound, Washington. He told me that he had a thirty-minute ferry ride on his drive home each day. For him, that thirty minutes was a wonderful time to relax and recharge his batteries after an exhausting day at the office. He also reported that the divorce rate in those communities across Puget Sound is much lower than in Seattle or elsewhere in the United States. That is a good example of built-in recycle time. Most of us, however, have to be a bit more creative.

But I also know what the wife's problem is, especially the younger woman who has small children. She's been with the children all day and wants an intelligent adult with whom to talk. Here he comes, and she has had one of those wonderful days only a homemaker can have.

The dog went rabid, the neighbor's crazy son (the one with the purple hair) broke both his legs jumping off the roof, and the garbage disposal is clogged up. On top of that, the washer won't wash and the dryer won't dry, and the repairman just made a hole in the roof while he was fixing it. And the litany of sorrows goes on and on, ad nauseum. And this has been one of her better days! So she's just aching to tell him all about it.

But, no! He doesn't want to hear. He's cold and surly. He nods and cuts her off in mid-sentence. She knows for certain now that the flame is dead. He doesn't love her anymore.

But wait. It's probably not what she thinks. He's not having an affair with his secretary or with the blonde at the sandwich shop. He has been in a battle, too, and he needs to cool down.

She needs to restrain herself. This is the best advice I can give a young mother. Give your husband at least a half hour to cycle down. And keep the kids away from him for a half hour if you can. Now I know that would be an enormous ministry of love, but he will love you for it, and it will make a lot of difference.

Time Planning

I would also encourage wives to do what we discussed in the last chapter: that is, to make time to sit down with their husbands and examine the various commitments that they've gotten themselves involved in over the past year and decide what they want to drop and what to keep.

Even though you may feel guilty about dropping some of the things you had committed to do, couples simply have to cut out clutter in their lives in order to keep creative time for each other. Many men and women have trouble saying no to all of the various activities and appeals for their time. But if they agree to all of them, the good becomes the enemy of the best, and little by little, the time they spend with each other begins to erode.

Just as wives need a day off, husbands need a day for recreation or sports or other activities of their own, a day when they don't have responsibilities as a husband, a father, or a businessman. A man will behave better if he has a chance to unwind that way. So I urge wives, don't begrudge your husband his golf game unless it starts at five o'clock on Friday night and ends at ten o'clock on Sunday night.

In fact, it is marvelously helpful if a wife will send her husband off to play golf, tennis, or whatever he enjoys doing, with her blessing. The fact that she recognizes his need for recreation and is glad for him gives him the freedom to relax and truly recharge. Nothing can destroy the fun as much as a wife saying, "There you go again! Deserting me and the kids for that @#*$! golf game!"

Some men, however, spend every spare minute playing golf or hunting or fishing or anything else that takes them away from the family. That sort of abdication is excessive and wrong. But if his hobby is not out of line, wives, let him know you support him. Encourage him.

Let him know you're happy that he can get out and relax. Unwinding will be much more enjoyable for him if he knows he is not going to be attacked for it when he gets home.

By and large, though, I think we have to be ruthless with our schedules. Take your calendar and sit down with a friend and say, "Please take a look at this and see if you think it looks sane or insane." Maybe your friend can help give you some objective feedback. The person may take one look at your agenda and say, "What! You've got all this to do? You're crazier than a loon!" If so, you probably need to make some changes.

One of the most valuable things I ever did was to study how I spent my time over two-weeks. From the moment I got up to the time I went to bed, I recorded everything I did in fifteen-minute segments. It wasn't easy, but it helped me get a realistic perspective on the way I was spending my time.

A friend went over it with me when I was finished. It's good to have someone with an objective viewpoint help you see what the study reveals. If you're like me, you will probably discover that you waste an incredible amount of time at those times when you think you are very busy. That study really helped me clean up the way I operate. I now get a lot more done in a shorter amount of time, and I have more leisure time.

The fact is, every one of us has twenty-four hours in the day—no more, no less. We have the same amount of time that Jesus had. We have the same amount of time as Einstein or Thomas Edison or Mother Teresa. If we're not getting as much done, maybe it's because we're not using our time as wisely. Regardless of our field of endeavor, our talents and skills could be magnified if we would simply use our time more effectively.

Three Basic Elements

There are three basic elements of effectiveness that will help you use your time and skills to your best advantage. These are very simple, but they should be considered when you plan anything: *time, personal energy,* and *resources.* Those three elements determine what we do in life.

What a lot of people don't understand is that imbalance in any of those elements will impact their potential success. They may have the energy, but not the time or resources. Or they may have the resources and lack the other two. When they have all three—time, energy, and resources—they're in the perfect position to accomplish their goals, small or large.

After I made that discovery, I gained much greater control over my own life. I became able to predict my potential success with all sorts of projects, and I knew how to decide whether or not to take on a demanding assignment.

For example, I had been teaching a two-hour class for laymen on Wednesday evenings at our church as part of the ministry series. After a while, I began to feel that my effectiveness was marginal, and my energy level dropped noticeably in the second hour. I had the resources, and I thought I had the time, but I discovered that I didn't have the personal energy.

When I thought about the situation in light of the three elements, I realized that after a full day of counseling, I simply did not have the stamina for a two-hour session, on my feet, in front of a large class of men and women. So I decided that, in the future, I would only teach a one-hour class. If it couldn't be taught in one hour, then I would not teach the class.

These elements apply to all areas of our lives: at home,

on the job, in our civic and social activities, and anywhere else we choose to be involved.

Husbands and wives need to encourage each other in
this area. Wives, let your husband know he needs to take
a serious look at his schedule. He cannot be Superdad,
Superprovider, Superemployee or employer, and everything to everybody. He may have to practice in front of
the mirror, (as I recommended in the last chapter), learning how to say "No, no, no!"

Business Fears

Fear of failure in business can be a tremendous problem for
men. So much of a man's ego is caught up in how he perceives that he is perceived by his peers. I say it that way
because our own perception may be inaccurate. But more
important than how a man is actually perceived by his
peers is how he perceives that he is perceived.

It is very important for a man to feel competent, that
he is doing a good job. When a man loses his job or goes
through a vocational change, it can be very traumatic.
And when a man is between jobs, it can be a tremendously unstable time for him.

It is heard that during the Great Depression, many
men who were unemployed, who had nowhere to go,
would get up at a regular time, get dressed, leave the
house, and go sit in the park. It was important for them
to be going and doing something, even if there was nothing to do. That behavior helped preserve many men's
sense of self-worth and dignity during those terrible
times. It is clear evidence of a man's need to maintain his
sense of equilibrium.

If your husband is going through a career change, he
will really need your understanding. Loss of a job, or
changing careers for any reason, can be very threatening

to a man. It is very important for him to know that his wife and family still have faith in him.

No matter how competent their peers may perceive them to be, all men go to work with a little bit of fear that somebody may find out that they don't know as much as everybody thinks they do. I recently read a newspaper article that suggested that as many as 90 percent of executives admit they are afraid, at least occasionally, that coworkers will find out they don't know as much as people think they do.

A wife's expression of confidence in her husband is a vital part of their relationship. A very important factor in a man's *fear of failure in business* is knowing that his wife will still love and respect him even if he is not as competent as his peers think he is; or *especially if* his peers and everybody else lose confidence in him.

Men and Money

What can a wife do to help her husband with financial pressures? One thing she can do is to simplify her lifestyle. It won't help much if the minute he gets home from the office his wife says, "Guess what Harry bought Sue for her birthday?" I've got news for you. He does not want to know.

If he says, "What?" out of kindness, and she tells him, "He bought her a new mink coat!" I don't care what she may say or what she means by her statement, I'll tell you what he hears. He hears her saying, "You are not an adequate provider." Even if she thinks she is just passing information along and she just wants to talk to him, he will interpret her remark as an expression that she feels he is not adequate. Comparing your husband with Sue's husband down the street really isn't going to help his ego.

Not every man has every gift. Some are handy around the house; others are absolute klutzes. Don't tell your husband how Harry fixed Sue's garbage disposal with a hairpin. He doesn't want to hear that, particularly if he is not "handy." You don't want to say, "How come you have a Ph.D. in electronics, but we have to pay an electrician forty dollars an hour to change a light bulb?"

Focus on your husband's strengths. We all have different strengths. Some grew up in a fix-it world where, if you didn't fix it, it didn't get fixed; others grew up in a world where you always hired somebody to fix things.

Stroke your husband for what he does well. It feels good when Jan says to me, sometimes as often as once or twice a week, "I really appreciate the fact that you work so hard to provide for me." She doesn't have to say that, but it means a lot to me to know that she notices and cares.

One of the most frequent complaints I hear from men in private counseling is that they feel unappreciated. It will not hurt you to tell your husband, "Thanks for going out there in the jungle to provide for me and the kids." When you say, "Thanks for all you do for us," you have said some of the most tender words of love he will ever hear. At least, that's the way he will hear it.

Unfortunately, we live in a time when enormous emphasis is placed on material possessions. A woman often feels a certain amount of insecurity about her appearance or her skills. I know the pressures on women these days and the need to be well-dressed and to present an attractive appearance. But if a woman's wardrobe and jewelry and beautiful possessions become her consuming passion, then she will place an incredible strain on her relationship with her spouse and increase the financial pressures on the family.

Somehow we have to learn that material possessions are not as important as we think. When parents come to me very upset about their kids' value systems, I simply ask them, "Where do you think they learned their values?" If you spend all your time thinking about a new house, a car, a boat, clothes, or some other possessions you just have to have, how can you blame your kids for demanding to have all the latest fashions and to follow all the newest trends?

Parents really start to see the truth when their kids move out and start their own lives. Have you ever noticed that kids today do not want to begin at entry level? They don't want to work patiently, learn a career, and pay their dues. Instead, they want to start where their parents left off. They want color-coordinated houses, with the latest high-tech facilities and electronic components, luxurious furniture, and everything it took their parents years to acquire. And they don't want to wait!

But many parents are guilty of the same kind of materialism. Because we are overly concerned with status, we spend much more money for things than they're really worth because of the label, the brand, or the impression they will make. That is just another form of covetousness. We can hardly blame our children for imitating our materialistic value system.

A couple sleeping on a $1,000 mattress does not sleep any better than I do on a $200 mattress. The couple who paid $20,000 to have their roof repaired doesn't stay any drier than the couple who paid $1,000 for the same job. And a $10,000 automobile may not have the style or the status of a $50,000 luxury car, but it will serve you just as well—it will get you where you want to go.

Believers should be concerned about susceptibility to materialism. The apostle Paul said that he had learned to be content in all things: in pain and in pleasure, and with little or much (see Philippians 4:11). I believe we must also learn those virtues, particularly when financial pressures start to build.

In order to reduce the pressures that we load onto ourselves, we should simplify our life-style. This means, out of love, reducing the material demands we make on each other. What good will it be if you have a wonderful life-style with all the latest creature comforts, but suddenly your husband has a cardiac arrest at fifty years of age trying to provide it for you?

What is more important to you, people or things? The Christian principle has always been that people should be most important. So one of the most loving things a wife can do for her husband is to help him find ways of reducing expenses and taking some of the inflation out of their life-style. Take some of the financial pressure off.

Husbands and wives are equally guilty of falling into the trap of materialism. Once you get caught, it is very hard to get out.

Problems with Self-Esteem

Low self-esteem does not generally rank quite as high on the men's list of concerns as on the women's, but it can be a problem whenever there is a high pressure environment and when men and women are struggling to maintain balance in their lives.

By and large, a man's self-esteem is tied to how he performs in two basic areas: his career and his sex life. One of the most sensitive things I ever heard came from a woman who told me, "I always make it a point to seduce my husband on the night he pays the bills." Now there is a very savvy woman!

I don't know if that's the way it ought to be, but for

many men, masculinity is tied to those two areas. A wife who loves her husband, and who sees him doing battle every day in the business world, can provide reassurance and affirmation for him through their sexual relationship.

It is just as important for a man to feel that he is attractive to his wife as it is for a woman to feel that her husband finds her attractive and sexually appealing. In fact, I think it is healthy for the wife to take the assertive role in lovemaking from time to time.

You may recall the name Marabel Morgan, a writer whose book shot up to number one almost overnight. Did you ever wonder why she was so successful with her book, *The Total Woman?* It sold something like five million copies! I think the reason is quite simple. In that book, she gave Christian women permission to be seductive to their husbands. That was her secret.

All of these issues are matters of concern to the husband-wife relationship. The exercise at the beginning of this chapter simply helped point out which issues concern us most, and much of our behavior in marriage is shaped by the hopes and fears that come from such concerns.

As we recognize the unique differences between men and women, and as we explore the various barriers to effective communication in marriage, it is equally important to understand that our hopes and fears in marriage are really very much alike.

Both husbands and wives want a loving environment in the home; both want to sustain an atmosphere of mutual support; and both want some degree of peace and joy, especially if there are children. The common concerns of men and women make those things very clear. If they recognize that they have mutual goals, then why can't husbands and wives simply cooperate and work together to build solid and lasting Christian homes?

However hard it may seem at times, and however dismal the failures of the past, it can be done. We have the tools, we have the knowledge, and with the grace of God, we can have all the resources we need.

As we turn to the final pages of this book, I hope you are beginning to see the design of a healthy Christian marriage taking shape. I hope you see how the simple decisions you make can be the springboard to genuine peace and harmony in the home.

Now that we have taken a broad look at the issues, along with some of the risks and opportunities, let's examine the process of putting it all together. In the final chapter I would like to explore a couple of the fundamental issues that help to determine if we can, in fact, get there from here.

TEN

Putting It All Together: Or How Do We Get There from Here?

Harmony in marriage is such an important goal! Yet, when we examine the innate differences between men and women and when we see all the forces in our society trying to pull husbands and wives apart, we have to wonder if harmony is even possible.

The statistics on divorce, the legacy of the war between the sexes, and even the jokes we hear about marriage make some very loud statements about the dangers. But there are many good reasons for believing that successful marriages are possible.

For one thing, there is the mandate of the Scriptures that we establish our homes in love and harmony. Christ and the apostles would never have commanded us to establish our homes in love if it were not possible or desirable.

Nevertheless, I fear that a lot of the advice we get from psychologists and from authors about harmony in marriage sets up false expectations. In fact, some Christian authors are just as guilty as the trendy pop psychologists in leading people to believe they can just throw a switch and overnight discover this wonderful intimacy and oneness in marriage.

One of my own fears in writing this book is that some people may latch onto one or two points I have made here and decide that this is precisely what his or her spouse ought to do. I know that some books have created the illusion that there is some magic formula for success. Like a fad diet, those books make couples think they can discover five magic steps to marital bliss. That is another example of nonsense, and it can be a real danger for many couples. I hope every reader of this book understands that the process to happiness and unity in marriage is never by rote, and it is often complex.

Overcoming your differences and discovering how to care for the well-being of your loved ones must be learned. And it will involve change. To take meaningful steps toward harmony means being willing to modify your natural behavior in order to give love and to build the marriage bond.

Here's another warning: you cannot change your spouse; you can only change yourself. Maybe you know the serenity prayer, used by Alcoholics Anonymous and others: "God grant me the serenity to accept the things I cannot change, the courage to change the things I can, and the wisdom to know the difference."

In chapter 2, I stated that the perfect union of a man and woman is a powerful equation, but that the two elements of the equation are also unique and independent by nature. One element cannot speak for the other one or change it unilaterally.

You cannot speak for your spouse, but what you can

do is work on improving on your side of the equation. There's no guarantee that your husband or wife will change. But I guarantee you that there will be no meaningful change until your spouse can see positive change in you.

Given that reality, I would like to explore the idea of change in greater depth and then talk about restoration and forgiveness. It seems to me that these are necessary components of any marriage in the 1990s and perhaps the most important skills we will ever have to acquire.

Making Positive Change

How does change really take place? First, we need to understand that there are a number of obstacles to change. First, *change is scary.* When somebody says, "I can't change," he or she is really saying "I don't want to expend the effort or do the work it will take to change." The prospect of changing is frightening and intimidating.

In counseling, I call this concept "the agony of the familiar." I think that often we would rather remain in our agony with what is painful and hurtful (if it's familiar) than to face the threat of whatever the change may entail, however good or valuable it may potentially be.

We should also recognize that *change is slow.* People simply do not change their behavior or their essential nature rapidly. In fact, one reason people don't get more help from counseling is that they don't stay in the process long enough to make significant change.

The third obstacle is that *change is painful.* One reason for this is that we are creatures of habit. Somewhere between 90 and 95 percent of everything we do, we do habitually; that is, by habit or reflex. So changing a person's behavior means modifying habits and the deeply ingrained patterns of action and response.

Somebody said, "Habits have a life of their own, and they die slowly." I think that is true. Not only do they have lives of their own, but they also fight for their right to exist.

Early in this book I referred to the problem of determining how much of our behavior is *nature* and how much is *nurture*. Clearly, that is a crucial issue when it comes to the need to make elemental changes.

If your behavior is your nature, you won't change. You cannot change the very nature of the way you are made. But all through this book we have talked about the importance of developing certain skills and patterns of responding—those things can change.

We may not be able to change the fact that men fear closeness and women fear distance, but we can certainly change some of the habits and response patterns that men and women use.

Before we can implement change, we have to recognize these three obstacles: change is scary, it is slow, and it is painful. Then, after we have agreed on the importance of making fundamental improvements in our lives and our marriages, we must determine how we can overcome the liabilities and accept the positive benefits of change.

I tell couples in counseling that to bring about genuine and lasting change normally takes a year. It takes about six months to break a habit and another six months to install another (and hopefully better) habit in its place.

As I have noted in previous chapters, making positive changes in my own marriage was not always easy. When I recognized my need to change my conditioned responses to Jan, or to improve my behavior toward her, I was cuing myself, making notes to myself, and using a variety of simple tricks to modify my normal behavior. It took time and effort to move from that stage to the point where the new response became natural and habitual.

From a biblical perspective, there are two basic ways that positive change can come about. The first is what I call the Romans 12:2 concept. You recall the verse: do not be *conformed* to this world, but be *transformed* by the renewing of your mind. *The Living Bible* renders the verse: "Don't copy the behavior and customs of this world, but be a new and different person with a fresh newness in all you do and think. Then you will learn from your own experience how his ways will really satisfy you."

For positive change to take place, it is imperative that you change your way of thinking. You have to have what Stephen Covey, author of *The Seven Habits of Highly Effective People* (S&S, 1989), calls a "paradigm shift," a different way of thinking. This is also very much what spiritual conversion is all about.

When you make an elemental change in the way you see things, you begin to see the events of your life through a different lens, a different paradigm, but you don't do it overnight.

In Proverbs, Solomon said, "As a man thinketh in his heart, so is he" (23:7). Long before Norman Vincent Peale talked about *the power of positive thinking,* Solomon was (through the spirit of God) giving us that truth. That is a very biblical concept: if you think positively, you will be a positive person.

It is interesting to observe how the wisdom of Solomon (3,000 years old) and the Romans 12:2 concept compare to what we know today as Rational Emotive Therapy (RET), a theory developed by Albert Ellis, who was anything but a believer. The RET theory is commonly used today and it basically says that "stinking thinking leads to stinking living."

The person who says "I can't help the way I feel" doesn't realize that how people think determines how they feel. I can only reiterate what I said earlier, that the way you talk to yourself about the events in your life is often more important than the events themselves.

The diagram I commonly use to describe this process indicates how we respond to the various events in our lives. When an event occurs (when something happens to you in your life), the first thing you do is talk to your-

THE EVENT / RESPONSE CYCLE

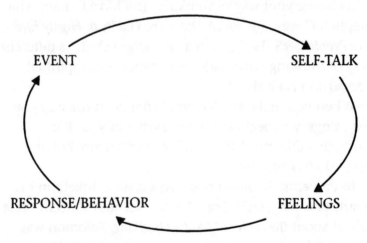

self about that event. The way you talk to yourself will determine how you feel about that event. Your feelings then will determine how you behave in response to the event; and that, in turn, will precipitate another event. Your response then becomes an event in somebody else's life, and that starts the cycle all over again.

To make positive change, we have to interrupt this cycle at the point of self-talk. In biblical language, we are

transformed by changing our accustomed pattern of thinking: that is, by the *renewal of our mind.*

Consider this example. If a man goes to work and
gets fired, he will certainly talk to himself about that
event. If he decides, "It looks like one other person has
found out how incapable I really am!" he will go away
feeling neglected, dejected, rejected, sad, guilty, and so
forth.

But he could also say, "Well, God has closed this door.
He must have a reason. I wonder what new door he is
going to open up to me now?" With that reaction, he will
go away feeling excited and exhilarated, anxious to get
back on the street to find out what's in store for his life.

The event was the same, but the feelings and responses
were very different. That's one of the ways we make positive change. We have to change the way we think.

Life's Layering Process

Our thought processes are largely determined by parenting and conditioning, along with all the subsequent layers of our lives that become part of the way we think. But
the main point is that change takes place at the level of
self-talk. How we respond, how we feel, and how we react
all derive from how we think about the events of our
lives and how we talk to ourselves about them.

In therapy, we often have to go back and help people
look at the preconditioning and the patterning in their
pasts. Those things—what we call their "scripts"—and all
the messages they have received in their lives, determine
their feelings and interpretations of their life events.

When the repair process begins, it's like cleaning out
the filter. We have to make some essential repairs and
adjustments. Attitudes and patterns of response may

need a little work, but then the healing process can begin. That's one way of thinking about change.

The other way is to go back around the same circle, in the diagram above, in reverse. Thus you would have an *event,* a *response, feelings,* and then *self-talk* about the event. When you go that direction, you get into what psychologists call "behavior modification." But you are also into what Jesus said about obedience.

Scripture says if your enemy is hungry, change your behavior: go feed him (Romans 12:20). He didn't say to wait until you feel warm and fuzzy. Unfortunately, our generation is very feeling-oriented. We wait to act until we feel a certain way.

If you go around the circle counterclockwise, you will begin to feel differently toward your enemy; you will begin to talk to yourself differently about your enemy. That's another way that fundamental change can take place.

I quote Scripture in this book because I am trying to encourage people to be obedient to the Scripture. Whether you feel like it or not, act loving toward your husband or your wife simply because you want to obey God. If you do that long enough, an interesting thing will happen. You will begin to feel differently toward your spouse.

Try this approach and see if it doesn't make a dramatic change in your own marriage (or dating) relationship for the better. In fact, I would like to recommend some very practical and loving things you can do for your spouse. These aren't generalities, they're very specific.

The following lists come from the book *Living Together* by Mort Katz. I think these are practical and loving suggestions.

A WOMAN'S GUIDE TO PLEASING A MAN

Be interested in his work and its meaning to him.

Tell him he looks handsome when he looks handsome.

Show interest in his wardrobe if it is important to him.

Be aware of what makes him feel happy.

Be aware of what makes him feel unhappy.

Know what sports he enjoys and learn to understand them.

Get him gifts related to these sports.

Tell him (every day) what you admire and appreciate about him.

Help him to understand a woman's need to be appreciated.

Let him cry, for whatever reason, when he needs to cry.

Give him time to be with himself when he needs it.

Help him understand a woman's need for physical and emotional gentleness.

Be a good listener—particularly when he needs to talk about his problems.

Ask for his opinions about your wardrobe and be guided accordingly.

Always try to be punctual.

Express happiness for his joy.

Express sorrow for his pain when he hurts.

Surprise him occasionally with a love note or sweet card—sent by mail.

Try to cook the things he enjoys.

Give him plenty of room to make his own constructive decisions.

Offer suggestions when he needs them.

Consult him before inviting guests to dinner or accepting invitations.

Never criticize him in the presence of others, whether constructive or not.

Show an interest in his friends.

Don't compare him unfavorably with other men.

Include him in your home planning.

Share laughter with him.

Be thoughtful.

Share your feelings with him openly.

Ask him tenderly if he wants to make love.

A MAN'S GUIDE TO PLEASING A WOMAN

Listen carefully to her when she is talking.

Show interest in what she is saying and look into her eyes when she is speaking.

Admire the things that she does well and offer suggestions when she seeks them.

Tell her how, or in what ways, she makes your life joyful.

Express sorrow for her pain when she hurts and express happiness for her joy.

Be aware of what makes her happy or unhappy.

Learn how she expresses herself physically and emotionally and respond accordingly.

Learn what her needs are and try to fulfill them when possible.

Let her cry when she needs to cry, for whatever reason, and console her when she wants to be consoled.

Be supportive of her need for new activities, and encourage such efforts.

Show an interest in what she is wearing.

Tell her she looks beautiful when she looks beautiful.

Be interested in her work and its meaning to her.

Help her feel that her work is as important as yours.

Write a love note to her and let her find it unexpectedly.

Purchase a sentimental card and mail it to her.

Remember that small presents have an intimacy.

Remember her with gifts on specific dates and surprise her with spontaneous gifts such as tickets to a musical, or the theater, or take her out to dinner on no special occasion.

Call her from work for no special reason, just to let her know that she is on your mind.

With meaning, always tell her you love her—she never tires of hearing it.

Explain clearly and specifically to her what your feelings of joy and pain (physical or emotional) are about.

Share family decisions with her.

Consult her before inviting guests to dinner or accepting invitations.

Don't criticize her in the presence of others, whether constructive or not.

Show an interest in her friends.

Help her to understand your hobbies so she can develop an interest in them. Show interest in her hobbies.

Help her with domestic responsibilities when she needs help.

Give her time to be alone when she needs it.

Share humor with her so that you can laugh together.

Respect and appreciate her efforts to be a loving and helpful spouse.

Show that you enjoy doing something for, or with, her.

Don't compare her unfavorably with other women.

Share the joyful or painful feelings with her that you experience in your work each day. She may not understand the technical aspects of your work, but she wants to know about what you feel inside in relation to your work.

Remember that women love to feel remembered with a gift when you've been away.

Ask her tenderly if she wants to make love.

For those who like *To Do* lists and for those who want to exercise Ephesians 4–5, just out of obedience, these are some positive steps for putting love into action.

Many times in counseling I will give couples what we call "courtship assignments" to do each day. I tell them to do something nice to make their spouse's day each day until I see them again. They can't tell their spouse what they're doing. It has to be something they can do quietly and without broadcasting it or gloating over it.

Most of the time when they come back for their next visit, the whole tone of the counseling session changes. Because they have been behaving differently, they start to feel differently.

Sometimes they may come in accusing each other, saying, "The only reason you did that was because Jim told you to do it!" So I have to remind them that that is the way we change.

When a wife tells her husband, "I expect you to do nice things for me because you *want to do it*," that contradicts what we know about the way people make positive change. Change is a conscious, deliberate effort: you have to work at it. It is going to feel weird at first—like changing a bad golf swing.

If the club pro tells you to try a new stance or a new swing, you may feel like you have a piano bench tied to the end of your club. The natural thing would be to revert to your old habits. But if you practice the new, positive behavior faithfully, in time it will become habitual. The new, positive behavior will replace the old, negative behavior, and eventually you will wonder how you ever thought the old way was better.

That is also the way we change in obedience to Scripture. The passages we have examined are not there to make the Bible appear pious and religious; they're there because God is telling us how to behave, regardless of how we feel.

If people understand that there are positive actions they can take to make their spouses feel loved, and if they can understand that God expects them to behave with love toward their spouses, regardless of how they feel, then change is not only possible, it is predictable, and it is exciting.

Learning to Forgive

No matter how good we are at learning new habits and conditioning our responses, no marriage can survive without burying the old animosities and suspicions that may have accumulated over the years. Along with change there must be forgiveness.

No marriage can survive without a lot of forgiveness, for in any marriage, husbands and wives will unintentionally, and sometimes intentionally, hurt each other. There is a lot of truth to the old song "You Always Hurt the One You Love." A person with whom we have a large emotional investment has enormous power to hurt us—intentionally or unintentionally.

Ephesians 4:32 says we should "be kind to each other, tenderhearted, forgiving one another, just as God has forgiven you because you belong to Christ" (TLB). If God has the grace to forgive you for all your sin and error, shouldn't you be gracious enough to forgive a loved one who may have hurt you in the past?

That is one of the greatest advantages of a Christian marriage. First, we have a model of forgiveness; and second, we have experienced forgiveness. It is easier to forgive if you have been forgiven. I can counsel an unbeliever to forgive someone else, but he does not have the model or the experience of forgiveness. Christian couples should cling to this advantage.

Do you recall the story in Matthew 18:21-35? That's where Jesus told the parable of the servant who was forgiven by his master for a very large debt but then refused to forgive another man of a much smaller debt. When the master found out what the servant had done, he had the unforgiving servant punished until he could pay the debt he owed. Jesus ends the passage by saying, "So shall my heavenly Father do to you if you refuse to truly forgive your brothers" (TLB). That is a stern warning that should be taken seriously.

The Three R's

It is easier to talk about forgiveness than to do it. I don't know what pains and indignities you may have experienced from your spouse—or perhaps from an ex-spouse—but first I want you to consider some alternatives to forgiveness. I call these the three *R*'s of marital strife.

If you don't forgive, what are your options? One is *restitution*. You can demand restitution from your spouse.

Have you ever thought what that really means? Few sins can really be paid for, so seldom do you, the victim, have the advantage or the power or the leverage to demand payment.

Some things just can't be paid for. How do you pay for a broken home? How do you pay for a ruined reputation? Sometimes repayment is impossible.

A second option would be *revenge*. If you can't get repayment or restitution, you may feel that you just want to get revenge. Often in divorce settlements people go to incredible lengths to do just that.

A few years ago, I was counseling a woman whose husband had had an affair. After we talked about the problems and the therapy that would be needed on both sides, I asked her to pray with me, to pray for her husband, and to forgive him so that the healing process could begin. She was having great difficulty with the process, and in the middle of the prayer she just stopped and said, "I can't forgive him. I don't *want* to forgive him!"

She would rather keep that anger and unforgiveness as a club over her husband's head. Obviously, there was no hope for restoration or healing in that relationship until she could give up her desire for revenge.

The third option is *resentment*. This really amounts to hatred. If you can't get restitution or revenge, you can at least have the wonderful satisfaction of hating the wretch. Of course you can! You can nurse a grudge until it grows into full-blown hatred. You take the risk that hatred will sour you into a suspicious, bitter, unforgiving, caustic cynic.

Hatred causes men to lose friends, merchants to lose customers, doctors to lose patients, attorneys to lose clients, and ministers to lose parishioners, to say nothing of the fact that it can elevate your blood pressure, upset your digestive system, ulcerate your stomach, bring on a nervous breakdown, and maybe give you a coronary. So go ahead and boil inside; but know that it is a slow form of suicide.

If you get all steamed up with resentment, an explosion is inevitable. If you do a long, slow burn, you hurt no one but yourself. A man or woman who broods over wrong, poisons his or her own soul.

Restitution is impossible, revenge is impotent, and resentment is impractical, so what do you do? The only logical choice is forgiveness. Consider some of the things that have been said about hatred, anger, and the need for forgiveness.

General James Oglethorpe once said to John Wesley, "I never forgive." To which Wesley replied, "Then I hope, Sir, you never sin." Even the Lord's Prayer makes this principle clear: "Forgive us our debts as we forgive our debtors" (Matthew 6:12). God forgives us to the degree that we are forgiving to others.

George Herbert once wrote, "He who cannot forgive others breaks the bridge over which he, himself, must pass if he would ever reach heaven; for everyone has need to be forgiven. The man or woman who refuses to forgive will not be forgiven, for they have cut themselves off from love and mercy."

Clearly forgiveness is necessary, but maybe we need to look more closely at what it is and what is involved in forgiving someone. First, let me say what forgiveness is *not*.

Forgiveness is not simply looking the other way when wrong is done. Forgiveness never just winks at or overlooks a hurt. It never makes light of a wrong. In the language of today, you don't just "blow it off."

Forgiveness is not some kind of pious religious pretense that evil is not really evil and hurt is not really hurt. Forgiveness is not being polite, tactful, or diplomatic in the face of wrong.

Forgiveness is not simply forgetting. I do believe that when you forgive you may eventually forget, but forgetting is not necessarily forgiving.

Often when dealing with serious and complicated issues, such as incest and abuse, the brutality is so bad and the wounds so deep that the victims often forget. They block out the pain, but they have not forgiven. In those cases, there has to be therapy to bring the hurt back up to the surface so they can confront it and then forgive.

Forgiving is never simply looking away from wrong or ignoring it. To overlook evil is basically dishonest, and that cannot be the aim of forgiveness.

David Augsburger, in *Freedom of Forgiveness* (Moody Press, 1970), has written that "forgiveness chooses to hurt, to suffer, and to voluntarily accept undeserved suffering: that is, suffering I could have avoided, suffering that rightfully belongs to some other person."

Another way of saying it: "In forgiveness you bear your own anger, in wrath at the sin of another. You voluntarily accept responsibility for the hurt that a person has inflicted on you." This author says that the man or woman who forgives pays a tremendous price: "You pay the price of the evil you forgive."

If the state pardons a criminal, Augsburger suggests, society bears the burden of the criminal deed. If I come into your home and break a priceless heirloom that you treasure and you forgive me, you bear the loss and I go free. Suppose I ruin your reputation. If you forgive me, you must freely accept the consequences of my sin and let me go free.

In that light, forgiveness is truly a powerful act, an act of almost divine proportions. No wonder it demands an act of selfless will; no wonder it is the central act of God's own plan of redemption.

Four Stages of Forgiveness

Lewis Smedes, author of the book *Forgive and Forget* (Harper Religious Books, 1984), says there are four stages of forgiveness. These are very useful for marriage, so I would like to review them. He says that first of all *you hurt*. Until you hurt, you have not entered the forgiveness process.

Second, he says, *you hate*. People need to understand in marriage that hate is not the opposite of love. Hate and love are often very kindred emotions. In marriage, apathy is the opposite of love.

If a couple comes in for counseling and they're boiling with anger at each other, I can work with that. There are still grounds for reconciliation. Their anger is an indication that they still care. However, when they come in and one of them has completely lost interest and doesn't care anymore, there is little chance I can do much good for them. In most cases, that relationship is over.

Third, Smedes writes that *you choose to heal*. That means that you make a conscious choice to forgive. This is very close to my own definition of forgiveness: I give up my right to hurt you for hurting me.

It is important for all of us to recognize that forgiving someone is a process. We know that God's forgiveness is once and for all: when God forgives us, our sin is forgotten. But it is usually not quite that easy for men and women.

Remember the passage in Matthew when Peter asked Jesus how many times a man should forgive another man. Peter thought that seven sounded about right, but Jesus responded, "Seventy times seven" (Matthew 18:22).

I think that at least a part of what Jesus meant was that you may have to go through the process of forgiveness many, many times.

The first time you forgive someone it is a conscious act of the will, and you may have to forgive that person for many things, repeatedly. But you may also have to forgive him or her for the first offense, time and time again as well. That is part of the process.

I have counseled those who realized they were still bearing a grudge against another person even though they had already consciously forgiven them. They say, "I thought I had forgiven him for that." But something triggered a whole set of feelings.

I have to remind them that they are remembering the hurt they felt, and they are feeling all the related emotions of that experience. Most of the time that does not mean they have not forgiven the other person, though they may need to repeat the process of forgiveness anyway just to clear out the rubbish.

Couples who have struggled over some of these issues need the security of knowing that none of these emotions is necessarily fatal to a marriage. Yes, we all hurt each other, and we all get hurt. Pain is inevitable. At the same time, we all need to be willing to ask for forgiveness when we have offended our spouse; and more important, we all need to be capable of forgiving our spouse, whether or not we are asked for forgiveness.

When the feelings of pain return, we may have to purge them again and consciously let go of our right to hate or hurt the other person. But that is the process that leads to healing and to restoration in a marriage relationship.

The fourth and final stage of forgiveness identified by Smedes is that *you begin to see each other through magic eyes.* That means you see beyond the hurtful behavior of the other person to the source of hurt that may have caused that person, or at least allowed that person, to hurt you.

For example, a man whose father abused him begins to realize that his father was also abused as a child and carried those scars throughout his life. A woman whose husband had an affair recognizes that her husband had not wanted to hurt her, but he was nursing a deep emotional insecurity. This does not mean that these hurtful acts were all right: wrong is still wrong. But it means that beyond their awful, harmful acts, you see that they also need love, forgiveness, and healing.

Smedes's term *magic eyes* means seeing someone you once hated in a different light—from a new perspective. It means that the process of forgiveness is working. That new way of seeing is essential for healing in a relationship.

Someone has wisely said that "all of us need a garden where we can bury revenge and resentment. And in that sense, only the brave know how to forgive."

Author Laura Sterns said, "Forgiveness is the most refined and generous pitch of virtue that human beings can arrive at. A coward never forgives. It is not in his nature."

Lord Chesterfield wrote, "Little vicious minds abound with anger and revenge and are incapable of feeling the pleasure of forgiving their enemies."

Someone else wrote, "It requires only an ounce of grace and a thimble full of brains to hold a grudge, but to entirely forget an injury is truly beautiful."

Edwin Chapman wrote, "Never does the human soul appear so strong and noble as when it forgoes revenge and dares to forgive an injury."

And of course Jesus said, "Your heavenly Father will forgive you if you forgive those who sin against you; but if you refuse to forgive them, he will not forgive you" (Matthew 6:14-15, TLB).

In marriage, it is cheaper to pardon than to resent a wrong done against you. Forgiveness saves the expense of anger, the cost of hatred, the waste of spirit. Bitterness is a paralysis of the mind, soul, and spirit that freezes our reason, emotions, and responses, and affects our attitudes. It turns us cynical and uncaring, critical and caustic, and it enslaves us to our most damaging emotions. That is why forgiveness alone brings freedom in a relationship.

Love and Respect

When we examine the basic attitudes of men and women we cannot deny that we have a lot in common. In advising husbands and wives to take their differences seriously, I do not want to overemphasize the differences to such a degree that they ignore all the emotions, hopes, and feelings they share.

We all want happiness, peace, security, a feeling of worth, a feeling of support and mutuality, and someone with whom we can share our ups and downs. Obviously, there is a lot of shared territory between us and plenty of room for understanding and agreement.

In chapter 3 we reviewed the eight traits of a healthy marriage, and we saw the fifteen trends identified by Christian families as keys to a happy home. In chapter 4 we discussed the principles of effective communication; and in chapter 5 we explored some of the ways we communicate nonverbally.

We talked about intimacy, the sexual relationship, and some of the barriers to intimacy in chapter 6; conflict resolution in chapter 7. Finally, in chapters 8 and 9, we examined some of the specific felt needs of men and women.

When we boil it all down, even the most dramatic differences are not all that hard to see. We know that *women need love;* they need and expect romance in their marriage, and most women will give themselves unreservedly to the man who satisfies that essential need and emotion.

On the other hand, we know that *men need respect.* More than love or sex or any other emotional requirement, a man needs the respect of his wife and family, just as he seeks the respect of his peers. If that need is threatened, he can grow angry and difficult; but he will give himself unreservedly to the woman who helps him satisfy that essential need.

There are many other issues, and I have attempted to give some perspective to the ones I encounter most often in my own practice. But I hope you recognize that one of the basic aims of marriage is to satisfy the needs of your loved one and to be willing to make whatever reasonable compromises or sacrifices may be needed in your behavior to do so. And as we observed earlier in this chapter, we all fail, and we all need forgiveness.

What author Tim LaHaye called "the Act of Marriage" is a complex process and an incredibly comprehensive commitment. It is not limited to procreation and the rearing of children; it is not limited to romance; nor is it limited to a household or a job or the accumulation of property.

Marriage is a fundamental and holy union, a physical and emotional oneness created by God and commended by him so that we each—man and woman—complete and complement each other. When we do that, when we complete and fulfill our loved one as God intended, we also become the man or woman God intended us to be. Marriage, in that context, is a self-fulfilling act of love.

In closing, I would like to reiterate my comment in chapter 1, that if somehow, with God's help, we can begin to deal with our basic differences as men and women, and not simply deny them; and if we can again begin to recapture and practice the biblical mandate of loving and forgiving; then for the second time in the history of man we will have discovered fire.

May it be so.